🔲🔲🔲🔲🔲

# A MIGHTY FERMENT

🔲🔲🔲🔲🔲

THE MIRROR OF BRITAIN SERIES
*General Editor : Kevin Crossley-Holland*

# A
# MIGHTY FERMENT

🔳🔳🔳🔳🔳🔳

## BRITAIN IN THE AGE OF
## REVOLUTION 1750-1850

🔳🔳🔳🔳🔳🔳

David Snodin

ANDRE DEUTSCH

*For my parents*

First published 1978 by
André Deutsch Limited
105 Great Russell Street London wc1

Copyright © 1978 by David Snodin
All rights reserved

Printed Offset Litho in Great Britain by
Cox & Wyman Ltd
London, Fakenham and Reading

Colour plates originated by
Dot Gradations Ltd, Southend
and printed by Sackville Press Billericay Ltd

*British Library Cataloguing in Publication Data*

Snodin, David
　A mighty ferment. – (The mirror of Britain series.)
　1. England – Civilization – 18th century – Juvenile
　literature　2. England – Civilization – 19th century
　– Juvenile literature
　I. Title　II. Series
　942.07　　　　　DA485　　　　77–30398

　ISBN 0–233–96925–X

199283

᠖᠖᠖᠖᠖᠖

# CONTENTS

᠖᠖᠖᠖᠖᠖

᭒᭒᭒᭒᭒᭒

# ACKNOWLEDGEMENTS

᭒᭒᭒᭒᭒᭒

Grateful acknowledgements are due to the following for permission to reproduce the colour and black-and-white plates: The Lord Abinger, 31; Ashmolean Museum, Oxford, 34; British Travel Association, 7; A. F. Kersting, 2, 21, 22; Manchester City Art Gallery, 6; The Mansell Collection, 7, 8, 10, 12, 13, 14, 15, 16, 17, 18, 19, 37, 48, 49; The Museum of London, 9, 47; National Gallery, London, 1, 8; National Monuments Record, 46; National Portrait Gallery, London, 20, 30, 32, 33; Science Museum, London, 3, 11; Shakespeare Memorial Theatre, Stratford-upon-Avon, 28; Sir John Soane's Museum, London, 4; South London Art Gallery (photo: Tate Gallery, London) 2; Tate Gallery, London, 5, 6, 1, 5, 23, 25, 26, 27, 35; Victoria and Albert Museum, London, 4, 9, 24, 36, 39, 41, 43; The Walker Art Gallery, Liverpool, 3.

I wish to express my sincere thanks, too, to Moira Walters for photographing plates 29, 36, 38, 40, 42, 44 and 45, to John Goulder for photographing the Shelley portrait, to my brother Michael for his help and encouragement, to my father, to Duncan Campbell Smith and Peter Stothard for their close reading of the typescript, and finally to Pam Royds for her patience and support during certain birth-pains.

꙱꙱꙱꙱꙱꙱

# INTRODUCTION

꙱꙱꙱꙱꙱꙱

> There was a mighty ferment in the heads of statesmen and poets,
> kings and people. According to the prevailing notions, all was to be
> natural and new. Nothing that was established was to be tolerated. . . .
> The world was to be turned topsy-turvy.

THE critic William Hazlitt wrote those words in 1818. He was
specifically referring to an important decade in the world's history – the critical years which followed the French Revolution
of 1789. But Hazlitt's words can be widened in their application
and used to describe a longer period of time. Long before there
were any hints of revolutionary activity in France, Dr Johnson
made an observation that was not unlike Hazlitt's:

> The age is running mad after innovation; all the business of the world
> is to be done in a new way . . .

And in 1833, half-a-century later, and three years after
Hazlitt's death, the novelist Bulwer Lytton wrote:

> Old opinions, feelings – ancestral customs and institutions are
> crumbling away, and both the spiritual and temporal worlds are
> darkened by the shadow of change.

In 1849, the poet Matthew Arnold bemoaned the passion for
transformation that was still going on around him:

> But we, brought forth and rear'd in hours
> Of change, alarm, surprise,
> What shelter to grow ripe is ours?
> What leisure to grow wise?

Throughout the hundred years that are the subject of this book, radical change was a vital part of the political, social and cultural climate. And that is why I have chosen Hazlitt's phrase 'a mighty ferment' as my title.

The ferment was not restricted to Britain. It was a huge turmoil – a whirlwind which raged through most of Europe, demolishing traditions, values and institutions that had been accepted as indestructible for centuries. And because most of the world's other continents had already been, or were in the process of being, colonised by various European nations, the ferment reached out to encompass them too. Perhaps its most important effect outside Europe was the creation of a vibrant new nation in North America.

Modern historians look back on this tempest as being nothing less than the birth of the modern world – with its speed and bustle and thrust, its delight in progress, its faith in the value of freedom and democracy (and the countless interpretations which are given to those words), its bright opportunities, its hopes and its fears.

Britain's role in the ferment was considerably less bloody than that of other countries. There were no battles, no violent overturnings. No monarchs were toppled from their thrones. No revolutionaries or legislators were marched out in their droves to be executed. But it was a transformation that was no less exciting or important for that. It has come to be known as 'the industrial revolution'. Britain was the first country in the world to experience the transition from an agricultural, rural society to a society dominated by towns, factories and machines. This book is an attempt to describe that transition, and to say something about the way it affected the thoughts and feelings of those who lived through it – thoughts and feelings which, in many ways, remain the essentials of modern culture, not only in Britain, but throughout the world.

# BEFORE THE FERMENT

𑿁𑿁𑿁𑿁𑿁𑿁

*Mr and Mrs Robert Andrews* (see colour plate 1), painted by the young Thomas Gainsborough in the middle of the eighteenth century, captures the spirit of a society still unaffected by the mighty ferment that is the subject of this book. The atmosphere of the painting – serene, peaceful, content – is conveyed, not only by the quiet beauty of the landscape, but by the faces and bearing of the young couple. It is difficult not to envy them. They seem privileged and untroubled. It is also difficult not to feel rather small in their presence. Like the dog with an eager respect for its master, we have to look up to them, because there can be no question that they are looking *down* at us. Everything about them suggests a secure belief in their own superiority.

They can afford to feel relaxed and superior, because Mr Andrews is a landowner – the glorious landscape behind him is *his* – and in this pre-industrial world to own land was to have power. The landowning class was the governing class. The British parliament was composed entirely of landowners, whether they belonged to the true nobility who made up the House of Lords, or whether, like Mr Andrews, they were 'lesser gentry', in which case they sat in what was rather inappropriately called the House of Commons. They presided over local as well as national affairs. In his official capacity as Justice of the Peace, the landowner had control over the life of his neighbourhood, settling local disputes and bringing local wrongdoers to justice. More informally, he felt responsible for the general welfare of the men and women who worked on and around his estates, and he would occasionally entertain the community at his own house. He often earned the respect and affection of the locality for his efforts. The essayist Joseph Addison created a country squire called Sir Roger de Coverley, who typified the benevolent landowner:

> My worthy friend Sir ROGER is one of those who is not only at Peace within himself, but beloved and esteemed by all about him. He receives a suitable Tribute for his universal Benevolence to Mankind, in the Returns of Affection and Good-will, which are paid him by every one that lives within his Neighbourhood.

But even if the landowner was *not* a man who inspired affection – and many were less charitable than Sir Roger – nobody questioned his authority. Society at the time was controlled by what Dr Johnson called 'the fixed, invariable, external rules of distinction of rank'. In other words, it was a well-defined hierarchy in which everybody knew his place. A poor person – and most people were very poor – did not yet believe that he or she had a right to be anything *but* poor. The idea that all men were equal was unheard of, and the underprivileged majority were largely content to live and work within the limits imposed by their lowly station.

Most people felt that this state of affairs had been ordained by God since the beginning of time, just as God had ordained the wider, more wondrous, hierarchy of the universe as a whole. This universal hierarchy was known by early eighteenth century thinkers as 'the Scale of Being'. Alexander Pope, the greatest poet of this static and self-assured society, referred to a

> Vast chain of being, which from God began,
> Natures aetherial, human, angel, man,
> Beast, bird, fish, insect!

All aspects of life had a pre-destined part to play in this glorious arrangement. 'All are but parts of one stupendous whole,' wrote Pope, 'whose body nature is, and God the soul.' The wonderful pattern of nature itself was all the proof needed to convince men of the existence of a kind God whose wisdom in the way He had arranged the world should not be called into doubt.

There was nowhere better to experience the splendours of

nature, and therefore the goodness of God, than in the rich plenitude and beauty of the British countryside. 'In Courts and Cities,' Addison wrote, 'we are entertained with the Works of Men, in the Country with those of God.' An increasing breed of wealthy town-dwellers claimed to despise country life for being backward and unfashionable, but most of the gentry acknowledged the country's importance by spending only a few months of the year in town, and the remainder on their various estates.

The great majority of people knew nothing of town-life in any case. In 1750, out of a population of around six million in England and Wales, and ten million in the United Kingdom as a whole, less than a million lived in towns. Of these, more than half a million were Londoners. Bristol, Britain's second city, had nearly 100,000 inhabitants, and Norwich, the next largest town, had around 50,000. The towns of the Midlands and North – Manchester, Liverpool, Birmingham, Sheffield, Leeds and Newcastle – were growing, and growing quickly, but none of them yet had a population as large as that of Norwich. For the most part, Britain was a country of villages, hamlets and vast stretches of open landscape (see plate 1), and for most people the life of the countryside was the only life they knew.

1. Eighteenth century rural England: *Landscape near Woburn Abbey*, by George Lambert.

Only the rich travelled; and even they did not *enjoy* travelling, for the state of the roads was appalling, coaches were uncomfortable and liable to overturn without warning, and the risk of meeting highwaymen and foodpads with little regard for human life was a severe one. But the majority – the poor – lived, worked and died in the village of their birth, knowing nothing of the world beyond the immediate horizon.

Agriculture was the full-time pursuit of over three quarters of the British population. But even the major 'industries' of this essentially pre-industrial society were rooted in the countryside. The manufacture of wool – Britain's main export – was carried out in rural surroundings by independent spinners and weavers in their own homes. The weavers were full-time 'professionals', but spinning, which required little skill, was often performed by agricultural labourers, or their wives and children, as an extra source of income. The iron industry – second in importance to wool – required a greater concentration of labour, but it was still rural. Foundries had to be built by rivers, for water was their source of power, and they also had to be within easy reach of a convenient forest, because charcoal was needed for smelting. Coal-mining – Britain's third most important industry – also belonged to the countryside. The mines were small pockets of industry in a landscape dominated by agricultural activity. Other minerals – lead, tin and copper – were mined in similar circumstances. At harvest-time, as a sign of agriculture's significance, the workers in all these industries would leave their looms, or their foundries, or their seams, to help gather the crops.

But life for most Englishmen in this rural world was far from idyllic. The wages of an agricultural worker varied from place to place, but the average wage was around a shilling a day. Industrial workers earned more, but for most of the population a great deal of penny-pinching was required in order to make ends meet. The price of bread – a poor family's staple food – could fluctuate drastically according to the cost of wheat, depending on the quality of the harvest. Bad harvests also caused widespread unemployment, and in the industries trade-slumps had a similar effect. There was no such thing as security of employment, and although a man might well have a great deal of work on his hands at any one time, there was no guarantee that he would have any work at all at another. And when there *was* work, labour was hard and the hours were long. A fourteen hour day, for women and children as well as adult males, was not uncommon.

The most celebrated example of hardship in pre-industrial Britain is Daniel Defoe's description of a Derbyshire lead-miner's family who lived in a cave:

> . . . says I, good wife, why, where do you live. Here, sir, says she, and points to the hole in the rock. Here! says I; and do all these children live here too? Yes, sir, says she, they were all born here. . . . I asked the poor woman, what trade her husband was? She said, he worked in the lead mines. I asked her, how much he could earn a day there? She said, if he had good luck he could earn about five pence a day . . . Then I asked, what she did, she said, when she was able to work she washed the ore. . . . But what can you get at washing the ore, said I when you can work? She said, if she worked hard, she could gain three-pence a day. So that, in short, here was but eight-pence a day when they both worked hard . . . and all this to maintain a man, his wife, and five small children . . .

When he went to see the mine itself, which was little more than a series of deep narrow holes in the ground, and met the miner, who, to his surprise, 'brought up with him about three quarters of a hundred weight of ore', Defoe concluded:

> . . . we had . . . room to reflect how much we had to acknowledge to our Maker, that we were not appointed to get our bread thus, one hundred and fifty yards under ground . . .

But at least the family had the countryside, and a rural existence did have its advantages. Defoe pointed out that the family 'seemed to live very pleasantly, the children looked plump and fat, ruddy and wholesome'. And they did not seem to lack sustenance, however paltry their income:

> There was . . . a whole flitch or side of bacon hanging up. . . . a sow and pigs . . . a little lean cow feeding upon a green place just before the door, and the little enclosed piece of ground . . . was growing with good barley. . . .

Such conditions compared very favourably indeed with the existence that had to be endured by the poorer town-dwellers. In London, the rich were already moving out to the cleaner air of suburbs like Paddington, Islington, Kensington and Richmond, while the poor lived huddled together in the city centre. The streets were narrow, unlit, unpaved, and overflowing with sewage. The people lived in ramshackle weatherboarded back-to-back tenements, and the really poor were crowded into dank filthy basements without a stick of furniture. Disease was everywhere. It was said, and it was probably true, that three out of every four children born in London died before they were five years old. Conditions in the larger provincial towns were, if anything, even worse.

It was in the towns that the huge contrast between ostentatious wealth and desperate poverty was most immediately apparent. While the poor lived in cramped alleys, with the permanent threat of disease and death, the rich paraded up and down the wider, better streets. The poor were not blind to such a contrast, and occasionally a wild frustration would break out in the form of a riot, during which they would burn or plunder all that they could lay their hands on. More often than not, though, they would seek solace in petty crime and in drink. Writing of London, Henry Fielding estimated that 'the principal sustenance of more than one hundred thousand people in this Metropolis' was gin. The sale of gin was not restricted by licensing laws, and, in London alone, there were over six thousand drinking-houses where the opportunity to get 'dead drunk for tuppence' was available to anybody who happened to be passing by.

As a London magistrate, Fielding came into daily contact with hundreds of the city's poorer inhabitants, brought before him for countless crimes of violence and theft. Most of them, he claimed, were drunk. He tried to understand what drove them to such things, and he realised that the cause lay in the terrible conditions they had to endure. He appealed in a pamphlet to the more fortunate members of urban society to show some compassion for their less privileged fellow-citizens:

... if we were to ... look into the habitations of the poor, we should there behold such pictures of human misery as must move the compassion of every citizen here that deserves the name of human.

There was precious little pity in Fielding's day. People of all classes relished cruelty without conscience. Rich and poor crowded into cockpits to watch cocks tear each other to pieces and gamble on which would survive. Bear- and bull-baiting were equally popular examples of the Englishman's bloodlust in both town and country. Pleasure was also derived from watching the agonies of human beings. Public hangings drew large crowds of jeering spectators, and there was no shortage of executions, for the felonies punishable by death were numerous, ranging from murder to petty pilfering.

In an age in which brutality and distress were commonplace and even enjoyed, it was easy for the wealthy to turn a blind eye to the sufferings of the poor. And besides, most of them firmly believed that the lesser orders *had* to suffer. Any alleviation of their poverty or their general misery would only encourage them to be lazy and make them forgetful of their principal duty, which was to work very hard for the benefit of the fortunate few, whose duty was to govern and to enjoy their wealth and good fortune.

Enjoyment, in fact, was the rich person's primary occupation, and it was a time-consuming business. Horace Walpole, a wry and intelligent observer, complained of the burdens of pleasure:

It is scandalous, at my age, to have been carried backwards and forwards to balls and suppers and parties ... as I was all last week ...

Fashionable life in the country was slower, but no less dedicated to amusement. Hunting and shooting were the country gentleman's main pursuits. Horse-racing was also a popular pastime, and massive sums of money were won and lost with easy abandon at the race-courses in Newmarket, Epsom and Doncaster. 'The beginning of October,' wrote Walpole, 'one is certain that everybody will be at Newmarket, and the Duke of Cumberland will lose ... two or three thousand pounds.'

Careless extravagance was a sort of fashionable duty. Squandering huge fortunes without batting an eyelid was a way of becoming someone worth knowing. The amounts wasted on gambling, however, were paltry when compared with the sums the wealthy spent on building and 'improving' their homes in the country. Most of these glorious country houses still exist, and as we approach them through their carefully landscaped grounds, or walk through their long galleries and vast reception rooms, it is all too easy to forget the darker aspects of the age in which they were built. It is also difficult to think of them as homes, although that is of course what they were. In order to catch their true spirit we have to imagine them, not as the silently elegant museums they have since become, but as places which rang with the sounds of the gentry in their restless pursuit of pleasure (see colour plate 2) – the sounds of music, of dancing, of conversation over the card-table, of laughter into the small hours of the morning. We have to picture the landowner striding down the long corridors in his muddy boots, red-faced after the day's hunting, shouting for his dinner, with countless servants bustling to his commands.

But to a certain extent the country house *was* a museum, even in its day. It was a place to be seen, a massive status-symbol. It dominated the surrounding countryside, a magnificent declaration of its owner's wealth and importance. It was also a reflection of his taste, not only in the design of the building, but in the things with which he chose to fill it – his furniture, his porcelain, his silverware, the paintings and sculptures which adorned his galleries, and the books which furnished his library.

Writers, artists and architects in this age before the ferment depended on the pleasure-loving gentry for their survival, because it was only the gentry, with their wealth and their hours of leisure, who could afford the time and the money to patronize artistic pursuits. It is quite easy, when talking about the culture of the pre-industrial age, to make hardly any mention of 'the people'. Because, in the opinion of the cultured and fortunate few, the people were not significant. They were 'nobody'. Fielding wryly remarked that, to the man of taste and fashion, 'nobody' meant 'all the people in Great Britain except about twelve hundred'. Pope referred to this uncultured and uneducated majority as 'the senseless, worthless and unhonoured

BEFORE THE FERMENT

1. The gentry and the countryside: *Mr and Mrs Andrews* by Thomas Gainsborough.

BEFORE THE FERMENT

2. The gentry enjoying themselves: William Hogarth's *The Dance*.

crowd'. Culture was essentially 'aristocratic' – obediently reflecting the tastes and beliefs of a small, select audience at the very top of society.

As a guideline in matters of taste, the wealthy, and the artists and writers who served them, looked to the world of classical antiquity. They felt a close affinity with that world, because they thought of it as having been a 'golden age' similar to their own – an age of stability and self-assurance, in which man had been at peace with himself and with the universe. A solid grounding in Latin and Greek was a vital part of every fashionable young man's education, and he would spend the years after university on a 'grand tour' of Europe, which culminated in a visit to Rome, where he could study the ruins of classical civilization at first hand. When, on his return to his own country, he began to think of building a home for himself, he used the clean, elegant lines of the classical temple as his starting-point (see plate 2).

The essential feature of classical taste was restraint. Pope called it 'good sense'. It was 'of every art the soul'. In other words, it was not only a rule which applied to architecture but to poetry and painting as well. The cardinal rule of poetry, according to Pope, was to 'Avoid Extremes'. It was not considered

2. The country house: Holkham Hall in Norfolk.

acceptable to get carried away, to be showy, self-indulgent or
eccentric. The poetry of Pope and his contemporaries was a
conscious imitation of the literature of the age of the Roman
Emperor Augustus, during which poets such as Vergil, Horace
and Ovid had flourished – so it was called 'Augustan', and, like
the work of the Roman poets, its principal purpose was moral and
instructive. This did not mean it could not entertain or amuse.
But amusement for amusement's sake was not enough. Beneath
the chuckling – and there was a great deal – there was always a
stern lesson, and the lesson was 'good sense'.

The painters of the age also insisted on poise and proportion.
A balanced 'good sense' informs the most popular paintings of the
time – most notably the 'conversation pieces', with their atmosphere of domestic harmony (see plate 3), which became a part of
every artist's repertoire from about 1725 onwards. A brilliant

3. A conversation-piece by Arthur Devis: *William Atherton and his Wife*.

4. The darker side of the eighteenth century: Hogarth's painting of a madhouse. For an entry fee of two pence, fashionable visitors to the Bedlam lunatic asylum could watch the insane.

exception to the rule was William Hogarth, who preferred to depict the darker and less re-assuring side of mid-eighteenth century society (see plate 4). Significantly, his savage pictures were a little too close to brutal reality to appeal to fashionable taste. In this aristocratic culture, few people claimed that the arts were there to reflect reality – their function was to 'improve' reality, to paint out the inconsistencies in accordance with the prevailing preference for rule and order. So it is interesting that Hogarth found his true audience in the ranks of the middle class – merchants, manufacturers, 'professional' men and their families, town-dwellers for the most part, who had enough money to buy copies of his engravings, but who were not rich or 'cultured' enough to move in fashionable circles.

The same class also provided an audience for a new taste in literature – called, appropriately enough, the novel. The first

true English novel was Samuel Richardson's *Pamela*, published
in 1740. It broke completely new ground, because by the standards of the time it was emphatically *realistic*. Not only that, but
its chief character was a member of the 'unhonoured crowd' –
a young servant-girl.

The novel rapidly became accepted as a new art-form. In
1749, Henry Fielding, whom we have already met in his role as a
magistrate, produced what is still regarded as one of the greatest
novels ever written, *Tom Jones*, the story of a bastard boy whose
adventures encompass the whole span of mid-eighteenth century
England. In the first chapter, Fielding expressed his simple, but
challenging intention: 'The provision . . . which we have here
made is no other than HUMAN NATURE.' And that is what he gave
his readers: a sprawling, often hilarious, work that abounds with
'real life', with all its irregularities and extremes of feeling, filled
to the brim with an array of characters as amusing and alive
today as they were when they were first conceived.

With their new outlook and their new audience, both Hogarth
and Fielding helped to bring culture out of the calm interior of
the country house and into the crowded cramped parlour of the
ordinary man and woman. Their extraordinary appeal lay in the
fact that they were out to win hearts, not minds – the hearts of all
rather than the minds of the privileged, classically-educated few.
And their moral purpose was clear: to attack the sham and
cruelty of their age, and to stress the importance of kindness and
pity in a world in which such things were singularly lacking.

Nonetheless, they shared their contemporaries' pride in the
structure of British society as it was, particularly when compared
with societies abroad. And it was certainly true that, in com-
parison with France for instance, Britain seemed a paragon of
liberty and tolerance. In France the division between rich and
poor was an intractable gulf. The peasantry lived in appalling
conditions, and the nobility lived in a style so sumptuous that
few English gentlemen were wealthy enough to compete. And in
Britain there was a social intercourse between the upper and
lower orders that existed nowhere else in Europe. Sport, particularly, brought the classes together – especially the increasingly

popular sport of cricket. In 1746, when the County of Kent played an All-England side, the Duke of Dorset played for Kent. He let his gardener be his captain, acknowledging that, despite his lowly status, the gardener was the better cricketer.

What cause, then, was there for anxiety and disquiet in this land of peace, prosperity and tolerance? Of *course* there was poverty, and misery and pain and sickness, but was it right to question these things? Was it not better to smile and be content, to learn to live with the evil and the good as necessary parts of some great divine plan? Pope summed up the spirit of his times when he wrote with assurance:

One truth is clear, WHATEVER IS, IS RIGHT.

How long could such confidence last? If we look at the sky behind Mr and Mrs Andrews we can see a storm brewing. The clouds are about to break.

# THE AGE OF REVOLUTION

## I. THE SHIFT

IN 1770, Oliver Goldsmith recalled the village in which he had spent his younger days. It was a happy memory, prompted by a return there after many years of absence:

> Dear lovely bowers of innocence and ease,
> Seats of my youth, when every sport could please . . .

Since his youth, though, a change had occurred. The village was now empty, a desolate ghost of what it had been:

> Sunk are thy bowers, in shapeless ruin all,
> And the long grass o'ertops the mouldering wall . . .

*The Deserted Village* was a protest poem. Its subject was what Goldsmith called 'the depopulation of the country'. By 'depopulation', he did not mean that Britain's population was *decreasing*. From 1750 onwards, it began to grow at an unprecedented rate, so that by 1770 there were already a million more people in England and Wales alone than there had been twenty years previously. What Goldsmith was actually talking about was the depopulation of the *countryside*. The villages and rural communities which had characterized the British landscape since time immemorial were emptying. People were starting to move. They were beginning to search for work and happiness beyond the limited horizons that had satisfied their ancestors and even their parents. During the hundred years with which this book deals, movement was like a fever – more infectious and more incurable as the decades passed.

Before this great shift, farming, the occupation that employed the great majority, had been run on an 'open-field' basis. Each member of an agricultural community had his own piece of land. If he was reasonably wealthy, this piece would be large, a farm in the true sense, and he would employ his poorer neighbours to work on it. But even the poor labourers had a strip of land that was unquestionably theirs, upon which they could grow the crops and raise the stock necessary for their survival.

The problem with this system was that although it provided each man with a piece of land that he could call his own, it was not particularly efficient or productive. At the turn of the seventeenth and eighteenth centuries, the landed gentry, aware of the waste-fulness of the open-field system, started to buy up large tracts of the countryside and to 'enclose' the land by fencing it off. The enclosure system replaced the centuries-old world of the in-dependent yeoman farmer with that of the tenant farmer, who was responsible to his landlord, and who supervized a large farm consisting of several fenced fields.

If the landowners, in their attempts to buy the land, met with any opposition, they appealed to parliament, which was always willing to introduce an individual 'enclosure act' forcing the farmers to sell, whenever it was asked to do so. By 1750, over a hundred of these acts had already been passed. Between 1750 and 1760 well over a hundred more were enforced, and between 1760 and 1780 there were a further thousand. In 1801, a General Enclosure Act simplified the procedure, and by 1815 most of the British countryside was enclosed (see plate 5).

Historians have often criticized the landowners for being more concerned with personal gain than they were with the welfare of those they forced off the land in order to make agriculture a more efficient and profitable concern. So it is important to emphasize that, as a direct result of enclosure, the British countryside produced a greater quantity of better food for a growing popula-tion, and more people were able to live longer and healthier lives. But, whatever the arguments for and against, enclosure *did* create a huge mass of landless labourers who had at least once had a humble allotment of their own, but who now had nothing and

5. The British countryside in 1817: a painting by George Robert Lewis. The fields are enclosed.

nowhere to go. So where did they go? To begin with, they moved to areas which still practised open-field cultivation. But wherever they went, it was not long before enclosure caught up with them. There was finally no alternative but to leave the countryside altogether and to swarm into the towns in search of work.

By 1800, London had over a million inhabitants – twice as many as in 1750. But the towns of the Midlands and the North had grown even faster. Birmingham, with over seventy thousand inhabitants in 1800, had more than doubled its population in the preceding half-century. Liverpool, Manchester and Glasgow (all with populations of between seventy and eighty thousand) had trebled theirs.

But enclosure was not the only reason for the growth of the towns. From 1750 onwards, the major British industries experienced an extraordinary expansion, moving from country to town, and attracting more and more unskilled labour from the land as they grew in productivity and importance.

The story of the industrial revolution is a tale of energy and invention on the part of a number of remarkable individuals from a wide variety of backgrounds, ranging from the wealthy aristocrat to the humble weaver. But whatever their station in life, they shared a common motive. They realized that, in order to satisfy a rapidly expanding market for British products both at home and abroad, and to make that market grow even more, raw materials and finished goods would have to be produced and supplied more quickly and in greater quantity than was possible under the old methods of production and distribution. Radical improvements – in mining, in manufacture, in transport – were vital.

It was in an effort to increase the output of coal, for instance, that steam was first effectively harnessed as a source of power. Coal-mining was severely hampered by the problem of flooding until a certain Captain Savery of the Royal Engineers patented a pumping-engine designed to raise water from the pits by what he called 'the impellant force of fire' – by which he meant the power of steam.

Thomas Newcomen, an ironmonger, adapted Savery's idea and patented his 'atmospheric engine', in which a primitive steam-piston was used to rock a heavy wooden beam which controlled a pump in the mine-shaft. By 1750, the Newcomen engine had become a distinctive feature of the Northern British landscape.

James Watt, a mathematical instrument maker from Glasgow, took the idea a step further by conceiving of the 'separate con-denser', which meant that the constant cooling and re-heating required to keep Newcomen's steam-piston in motion could be avoided, and considerably less coal was needed to feed it. He had a second flash of brilliance when he decided to use steam-power for both the upward and downward strokes of the piston. New-comen had used steam for the upward stroke only, and relied on air pressure to push the piston down. With this innovation, Watt created the first genuine steam-engine. It was four times more efficient than Newcomen's, and it was rapidly adopted, not only for mining, but for raising water to turn the water-wheels in ironworks. It was perhaps this use that inspired Watt to come up with his third and most decisive masterstroke – the idea of making a steam-engine that would do the work of the water-wheel itself. By attaching a shaft from one end of a piston to the circumference of a wheel, he invented the rotative engine, patented in 1782. Now the steam-engine could be used, not merely for pumping water, but for turning machinery of all kinds, and the field of possibilities was wide open.

While the extraordinary potential of steam-power was being realised, significant developments were occurring in the woollen industry. John Kay's 'flying shuttle' effectively halved the labour-force required to weave wool. Whereas previously a loom had to be operated by two men, Kay's invention meant that one man could produce woven cloth on his own. And James Hargreaves' 'spinning jenny' replaced the old spinning-wheel and allowed one spinner to spin up to eighty threads at a time in his or her own home.

The jenny was used for spinning cotton as well as wool. In 1750 the cotton industry was still a relatively minor one, because a cotton yarn had not yet been produced that was strong enough to be used on its own in clothing. But Richard Arkwright's 'water frame' soon solved this problem. It was a monumentally important innovation, for cotton, despite the fact that the raw material had to be imported, was far cheaper than wool. There was an immediate demand for sturdy but inexpensive cotton clothes. When Arkwright's patent expired in 1785 the 'cotton boom' began. By the 1830s, cotton was the most important industry in Britain, employing over one and a half million workers, more than in any other single industrial occupation.

Arkwright's invention ensured the death of the 'domestic' textile industry, for it was far too large to be used in the home. Arkwright built the first cotton mill in Britain at Cromford in Derbyshire (see plate 6). In writing about the Cromford mill, an observer described an atmosphere that was to become increasingly familiar as the industry spread across the countryside:

6. *Arkwright's Cotton Mill at Cromford*, by Joseph Wright of Derby.

> I saw the workers issue forth at 7 o'clock . . . a new set then goes in for
> the night, for the mills never leave off working. . . . Every rural sound
> is sunk in the clamour of cotton works; and the simple peasant . . . is
> changed into an impudent mechanic.

The first cotton mills were dependent on rivers for their power, so they remained in rural settings. But in the 1790s, at the height of the boom, during which hundreds of cotton mills, large and small, sprang up in the North, the North-West, the Midlands and North Wales, the steam-engine replaced the water-wheel, and the new mills could be built away from the rivers and side by side in towns. By 1810, most of the cotton in Britain was spun in urban surroundings (see plate 7).

Because of the massive demand, the weavers of the 1790s, still working in their homes and in small workshops, enjoyed an un-precedented prosperity. But their happiness was short-lived. A clergyman and poet called Edmund Cartwright had already

7. Cotton comes to town. Mills in Manchester, 1830.

invented the steam-driven 'power loom', which was far too large for domestic use. Largely because of an understandably hostile reception from the weavers themselves, the power-loom took quite a long time to be accepted, but its advance was inevitable. By 1830, there were 100,000 power-looms in Britain, and the lively independence of life in the workshop had been replaced by the drudgery of life in the urban factory. At about this time, an anonymous Lancashire balladeer wrote:

> If you go into a loom-shop, where there's three or four pairs of looms,
> They all are standing empty, encumbrances of their rooms;
> And if you ask the reason why, the old mother will tell you plain,
> My daughters have forsaken them, and gone to weave by steam.

By then, Manchester, the centre of the cotton industry, and Liverpool, its main port, had around 200,000 inhabitants each – twice as many as they had had thirty years previously. By 1840, Manchester's population had increased by a further 50,000, and Liverpool's by still more. A Manchester doctor observed:

> New streets are rapidly extending in every direction, and so great already is the expanse of the town, that those who live in the more populous quarters can seldom hope to see the green face of nature.

Nature had also practically been obliterated in the iron and coal industries, for they too had experienced radical developments apart from the exploitation of steam. In 1709, at the Coalbrookdale ironworks in Salop, a Quaker ironmaster called Abraham Darby perfected a process that allowed iron to be smelted with coke rather than with charcoal. Until then, charcoal had been the only known form of fuel that did not introduce too many impurities into the iron, and it was for this reason that the industry had been dependent on the British forests. Darby's new method was only capable of producing cast iron – but in 1750, his son, Abraham Darby II, managed to produce the purer more malleable iron known as wrought iron from the coke-fed furnaces at Coalbrookdale (see colour plate 3). Freed from their need for charcoal, the blast-furnaces in the iron industry could begin to exploit the seemingly endless supplies of coal that stretched across Britain, and to forget the rapidly shrinking forests.

Because of the fortuitous arrival of the rotative steam-engine, the industry could also forget the rivers. The immediate result was a concentration of labour. The ironworks moved to the coal-areas, and the whole iron-making process, smelting, forging, and the mining of the coal now required for both tasks, could take place in a single community, often under the watch of a single proprietor. A huge labour-force was required, and densely-populated towns sprang up around the iron-works of Staffordshire, Yorkshire, Scotland and South Wales. In 1802, a traveller described the streets of the Welsh town of Cyfartha as

> close and confined, having no proper outlet between the houses. They are consequently very filthy for the most part. . . . The noise of hammers, rolling mills, forges and bellows, incessantly din and crash upon the ear . . .

As a monument to his family's contribution to the industrial revolution, Abraham Darby III built an iron bridge over the Severn in 1779 (see plate 8). It was the first iron bridge in history, and a triumphant demonstration of the way in which iron could replace wood as a basic material of construction – which is just

8. Abraham Darby's Iron Bridge.

what it was to do over the next fifty years. As the demand for iron grew, so the demand for coal increased with it. Between 1750 and 1850, the annual output of iron rose from 50,000 tons to over two million tons. Coal's tonnage rose from five million to fifty million.

Steam-engines were made of iron, of course, and they used coal – and by 1850, the steam-engine had become the prime mover in every branch of British industry. The most revolutionary development in steam-power – a development which swallowed a huge tonnage of iron and coal every year – was the railway.

Efforts had been made to improve transportation long before the railways came. From 1750, British roads underwent a remarkable improvement, largely through the encouragement of enterprising industrialists and through the brilliance of road-builders like John Metcalfe, Thomas Telford and John Loudon McAdam. By 1830, Britain was covered with roads which, for the

9. Stage coaches in a late eighteenth-century market town – a water colour by Thomas Rowlandson.

first time since the Romans, actually deserved the name. The new
roads helped to foster the idea of travel for its own sake. Moving
from place to place – at least for those who could afford it – became a pleasurable pastime rather than a burdensome require-
ment (see plate 9).

Good roads also had a beneficial effect on the distribution of
lighter industrial goods. The producers of heavier items and raw-
materials, however, preferred to transport their products by
water. It was this preference that led to the construction of a
complex network of canals from about 1770 onwards. By 1830,
there were three thousand miles of canal in Britain, connecting
the main industrial centres with each other and with the ports (see
plate 10).

1830 was the year in which the railways came, although
primitive horse-drawn 'railways' had been used in the coal-fields
since the late seventeenth-century. The man who is rightly given
most credit for replacing the horses with steam-driven locomotives

10. An aqueduct on the Bridgewater Canal, the first in a huge network.

3. An excited view of the Industrial Revolution: Philip James de Loutherbourg's *Coalbrookdale by Night*.

4. The greatest of British landscape painters:
John Constable's *Cottage in a Cornfield*.

was George Stephenson, a colliery engineer from Newcastle. His work caught the attention of a group of coal-owners who wanted to build a railway between the coalfield at Darlington and the coal port of Stockton. Opened in 1825 and masterminded by Stephenson, the railway used both locomotives and horses. It carried coal mainly, but it could also accommodate passengers. The success of the venture created a great deal of interest, and it was George Stephenson who was asked to construct the first all-steam passenger-carrying railway in the world. It ran between Manchester and Liverpool, and was opened with great ceremony in September 1830 (see plate 11).

Within twenty years of this grand opening, there were five thousand miles of railway in Britain, including the main trunk lines from London to the rest of the country. The new engines were quite capable of reaching the unprecedented speed of sixty miles per hour. It really was an extraordinary revolution. Families that had remained in one small area for generations were now given the opportunity to see more of the thriving nation to which they belonged, easily and cheaply, and it was an opportunity they were quick to grab. By 1850, ticket-sales had reached an annual average of eighty million. As people travelled, met, and talked, ideas, fashions and feelings circulated with them, and the barriers which had kept them apart for centuries crumbled. Quite suddenly, Britain was a much smaller place.

But in a sense the railways, and the effect they had, were only the dramatic extension of a phenomenon already in existence. People had been moving – reluctantly perhaps, but moving nonetheless – since the middle of the eighteenth century. The railways finalized this development. By the time they arrived, the great shift from country to town was well under way, and the feelings and thoughts of the thousands who had been a part of this shift were already very different from those of their rural ancestors. That air of quiet resignation that was the spirit of pre-industrial Britain no longer existed, at least not amongst the inhabitants of black, sprawling cities like Glasgow, Manchester, Liverpool and Sheffield (see plate 12). Their emotions and opinions were dark, discontented, increasingly noisy, and, to

11. The opening of the Liverpool and Manchester Railway, 1830.

12. The industrial heritage: Sheffield in 1850.

those who looked down from positions of privilege and ease, very
dangerous.

## II. NEW THOUGHTS, NEW FEELINGS

In the early stages of enclosure and industrialization, the labouring poor began to harbour new and angry thoughts. Understandably unconvinced by arguments about better cultivation, they
watched the landowners and tenant-farmers grow wealthy while
they, the poor, were forced to work elsewhere, and they started
to think of themselves as the victims of a conspiracy on the
part of the richer classes against the common man. And in industry,
arguments about the efficiency and productivity of the new inventions were hardly likely to appeal to those forced into unemployment by such developments. All that mattered to them was that
they no longer had work while their masters grew richer.

In the second half of the eighteenth century, the printed ballads
which had been sung and sold on the streets of villages and towns
since pre-Elizabethan days took on a new bitterness, cursing
the rich for exploiting the poor:

With the choicest of strong dainties your tables overspread,
With good ale and strong brandy, to make your faces red;
You call'd a set of visitors – it is your whole delight –
And you lay your heads together to make our faces white.

This particular ballad had a threatening chorus:

> You tyrants of England, your race may soon be run,
> You may be brought unto account for what you've sorely done.

In the scattered society of pre-industrial Britain, a man with radical thoughts, without the advantages of travel or the quick spread of ideas, lost and alone in the countryside, had no way of knowing how much other men were thinking along the same lines. But in the shift from home to factory, and from country to town, that man suddenly found himself working alongside hundreds of others who felt as rootless and as angry as he did. Brought together in their discontent, the labouring poor became that far more powerful concept, 'the working class'. An early historian of the cotton industry, Richard Guest, summed up this important change:

> The operative workmen being thrown together in great numbers, had their faculties sharpened and improved by constant communication. . . . from being only a few degrees above their cattle in the scale of intellect, they became Political Citizens . . .

Hard work for precious little reward had always been the lot of the labouring poor. But whereas they had previously regarded their condition as something ordained and unalterable, they now saw it as a positive injustice for which they could at last blame a particular individual – the employer. Manufacturers, clothiers, ironmasters and coal-owners became, in the eyes of their workers, cruel and impersonal tyrants, living in well-furnished and spacious houses while those in their employ had to make do with ramshackle tenements in narrow unhealthy streets.

Conditions in the factories helped to blacken the employers' reputation still further. Harsh fines were inflicted on those who arrived late for work or who, because the work was both tiring and dull, fell asleep at their machines. Nothing was crueller, though, than the exploitation of children. They had always been used for labour, but they had never had to endure such suffering as they did now. In 1833, Robert Blincoe, a manufacturer who had worked as a child in a cotton-mill, was asked by a parlia-

mentary committee if he would send his own children into the
factories. He answered:

> No; I would rather have them transported. In the first place, they are
> standing upon one leg, lifting up one knee, a great part of the day,
> keeping the ends up from the spindle; . . . then they are liable to have
> their fingers catched and to suffer other accidents from the machinery;
> then the hours is so long, that I have seen them tumble down asleep
> among the straps and the machinery and so get cruelly hurt (see plate
> 13).

In the coal mines, boys and girls as young as four years old were
made to work for an average of twelve hours a day. A Scottish

13. A child at work in a Manchester cotton mill in the 1830s.

girl, described as 'six years old, coal-bearer' gave an account of her labours to a parliamentary commission in 1840:

> Been down at coal-carrying six weeks; makes ten to fourteen rakes (journeys) a day; carries full 56lbs of coal . . . The work is na guid; it is so very sair (see plate 14).

The employers themselves found arguments to support the rigours they imposed. In 1776, Adam Smith, a professor at Glasgow university, published an important book called *The Wealth of Nations*, in which he propounded a philosophy of economics called 'the system of natural liberty' – better known as *laisser-faire*, or what the modern world refers to as 'free enterprise'. In Smith's view, the ideal society was one in which 'every man, as long as he does not violate the laws of justice, is left perfectly free to pursue his own interest in his own way'. This was the basis for the 'capitalist' economies practised by most countries in the Western World today, and that is why *The Wealth of Nations*, the first work to formulate the principles of capitalism, is one of the most crucial books ever written. Unfortunately for the workers of Smith's day, however, that important condition *'as long as he does not violate the laws of justice'* did not mean what it means today. Then, there were no laws governing the way in which a manufacturer should treat his employees, and he often used the idea of 'self-interest' as an excuse for the remorseless exploitation of those who worked for him.

14. A girl in a mine. This particular drawing, published with a report on the mines in 1844, caused many Victorian hearts to shudder with horror and guilt.

In 1798, Thomas Malthus' *Essay on the Principle of Population* was a further blueprint for cruelty. It raised a terrible, and totally new, spectre – the idea that the population of Britain was growing at such a rapid rate that the food required to keep this ever-increasing number of people alive would soon quite simply not be available. Malthus' answer to this problem was that if there was not enough food to go round, then a large section of the population, as a result of what he called 'the strong law of necessity', would have to starve, and that would act as a natural check on the increase of people. The awful truth, of which Malthus was well aware, was that such a necessity would be most 'severely felt' by the poorer members of society. Although he published his book out of a sincere concern for the future, his arguments were all too often used as a pretext for paying starvation-wages, ignoring the harsh quality of living- and working-conditions, and throwing people out of work without warning. If anybody complained, an employer could refer to Malthus, and claim that his actions were simply a part of the 'strong law of necessity'.

In the year of *The Wealth of Nations*, a startling event abroad helped to strengthen the revolutionary awareness that was growing amongst those who had to endure the new cruelties of the age. For it was in 1776 that the American colonies declared themselves independent from their British masters (see plate 15). After a war which lasted five years, they won their freedom. Their victory was a harsh slap in the face for the British government, but more significant than anything else were the first words of the Declaration of Independence itself:

> We hold these truths to be self-evident, that all men are created equal, that they are endowed by their Creator with certain inalienable rights, that among these are Life, Liberty and the pursuit of Happiness. That, to secure these rights, Governments are instituted among Men, deriving their just powers from the consent of the governed, that whenever any form of Government becomes destructive of these ends, it is the Right of the People to alter or to abolish it, and to institute new Government.

15. The American Declaration of Independence is read in
Philadelphia in 1776.

This clarion-call from across the Atlantic was very attractive
to those who were starting to realize that they lived in a society
in which the idea that all men were created equal was not at all
self-evident, and that they were ruled by a government that was
in no way representative of the people. Perhaps if a ruling body
could be instituted that was truly democratic, then something
could be done about the unjust suffering endured by the majority
of the population.

While the poor suffered, the privileged few were dancing and
spending with increasing abandon. Horace Walpole, himself a
lover of pleasure, wrote in 1777:

> One effect the American war has not had that it ought to have had;
> it has not brought us to our senses. Silly dissipation rather increases,
> and without an object.

A year later he wrote:

> Ruin . . . stalks on, and is not felt or apprehended. . . . Unless sudden
> inspiration should sieze the whole island . . . it will crumble away in
> the hands that still hold it.

Rioting was now a regular feature of town life, particularly of
London life.

> We are glad if we can keep our windows whole, or pass and repass un-
> molested. I call it reading history as one goes along the streets. . . .
> I do not love to think what the second volume must be of a flourishing
> nation running riot.

Fortunately for Britain, the real overturning happened in
France, in 1789 (see plate 16). The reception of the French
Revolution in Britain ranged from happy enthusiasm to horrified

16. The storming of the Bastille prison in Paris: the start of the
French Revolution.

fright. Its supporters believed that the French had created a
society based on complete equality overnight, and saw it as an
affirmation of their own beliefs. Its detractors believed in the
sanctity of society as it already existed, and felt that such a rapid
rush into equality could only lead to blind chaos. Of one thing,
though, there could be no doubt – the power of the lower orders,
if they put their minds to it, to overthrow the establishment
completely and irrevocably.

Intelligent men arrayed themselves on both sides. One of the
brightest was Edmund Burke, who published his *Reflections on
the Revolution in France* in 1790. Burke saw in the Revolution the
destruction of everything that was fine and valuable in society –
learning, grace, tolerance, order. 'Good order,' he wrote, 'is the
foundation of all good things.' He also believed that:

> Some decent regulated pre-eminence, some preference . . . given to
> birth, is neither unnatural, nor unjust, nor impolitic.

Burke's book, the final grand statement of eighteenth century
values, provoked a reply that heralded a new world – Thomas
Paine's *The Rights of Man*. Paine had experienced the American
Revolution at first hand, and his great work expressed, clearly and
persuasively, those truths that had been 'self-evident' to the
drafters of the Declaration of Independence, and which, merci-
fully, are self-evident to most of us now: that man is born free,
that no other man has the right to take his freedom from him, and
that everybody has the right, regardless of wealth or birth, to
have a say in the way a country is run. Within three years of the
book's publication it had sold 200,000 copies, a phenomenal
sale in a society in which most people were still illiterate.

In 1793, Louis XVI and his Queen were executed and the
French Revolution collapsed into the blood and confusion of the
Reign of Terror. Burke, in writing that 'a perfect democracy is
the most shameless thing in the world', seemed to have been
proved right. Britain went to war with France, and the war was
to continue, with the exception of a brief peace in 1802, for
twenty-two years. It began as a war against the revolutionaries,

and then became a fight against the aggressive intentions of a single figure – Napoleon Bonaparte. During the hostilities, loyalty to the British crown and the British way of life was paramount. Paine was in France for most of the war, and while he was there, copies of his book were burnt in his own country – not, ironically, by the government whose existence he had challenged, but by the people whose cause he had championed. Most of the British intellectuals who had welcomed the Revolution as the dawn of a new age suffered a serious disillusionment during the 1790s, and they either became ardent reactionaries or simply subsided into an inactive despair.

But it *had* been a dawn nonetheless, and nothing could now bring back the old world. War with France, after all, did not halt the progress of the industrial revolution, or the growth of the towns, with all the distresses they brought. The government of the 1790s was still terrified of the possibility of a working-class uprising, and it passed several repressive measures, including the suspension of Habeas Corpus, an action which gave magistrates the power to make arrests without having to give reasons, the Treason and Sedition Acts, and the 'Combination Acts', which were designed to prevent the poor from 'combining' in an attempt to fight for better conditions of work or for higher wages. These banned 'combinations' were, in effect, the first British trades unions.

The poet Shelley was to describe the war years as panic-stricken. 'Panic,' he wrote, 'like an epidemic transport, siezed upon all classes of men.' A particularly widespread cause for panic amongst the privileged classes was the fear that the poor were beginning to be over-educated. Actually, most of the poor could not yet read or write. But by 1800, several thousand 'charity schools', paid for by voluntary contribution and providing a free elementary education, had been built, and Sunday schools, offering poor children a few hours of learning a week, were a common feature in the industrial towns. The establishment of these institutions met with considerable opposition from the wealthy. They felt that a literate working-class would automatically be a rebellious one, and that the poor should be kept ignorant or they would start to have ideas above their station. Their fears, though, were hardly justified. Reading-matter in the charity and. Sunday schools was restricted to the scriptures, and the primary lesson was one which encouraged subservience. The opening hymn at a Sheffield charity school included the words: 'Make me temperate, chaste, meek and patient, true in all my dealings and content and industrious in my station'. And Hannah More, a leading figure in the Sunday school movement, made her own views perfectly clear when she wrote:

> Beautiful is the order of society when each, according to his place, pays willing honour to his superiors.

Education for the poor was deeply bound up with religion. Hannah More was an evangelical – the name given to an Anglican who believed that the church should make a determined effort to bring people back into its fold. Church attendance had fallen off during the eighteenth century, particularly amongst the poor. This was because the established Anglican church, too often represented by a snobbish parson reciting incomprehensible sermons in a boring monotone, was patently out of touch with the needs and feelings of the people, and because various non-conformist sects were wooing the people away. The most successful of these sects was Methodism, founded by John Wesley in 1738. Wesley's mission was not so much to bring people back to the church as to bring the church to the people, by travelling round the country and preaching in the open air, in words which the poor could understand. Between 1738 and 1791, the year of his death, this extraordinary man preached over 40,000 sermons, travelling 224,000 miles to do so. He encouraged literacy amongst his converts – 'Reading christians will be knowing christians', he said – and the Methodist Book Room in London published books and pamphlets which were, in Wesley's words, 'simply and nakedly expressed, in the most clear, easy and intelligible manner.'

Methodism did not die with Wesley. By 1800, it was a huge and powerful movement, and most of its members came from the ranks of the poor. Any large body of people, particularly of literate poor people, was a frightening spectre in the war years, and the Duchess of Buckingham spoke for many when she criticised the Methodist preachers for spreading doctrines which were 'repulsive and strongly tinctured with impertinence' and 'perpetually endeavouring to level all ranks and do away with all distinctions.' She was wrong, though. Ideas of rebellion could not have been further from the average Methodist's heart. Wesley's own view of the world was unrelentingly conservative. 'The greater the share the people have in government,' he wrote, 'the less liberty . . . does a nation enjoy.' In his view, the way to salvation was through hard work and subservience.

But without Methodism, and without the charity and Sunday schools, the *Rights of Man* would not have enjoyed such a wide readership. Neither would the host of radical pamphlets that followed its example, or the 'democratic' newspapers that appeared in the provinces – all of which, as far as the government was concerned, existed for the sole purpose of inciting their readers to rebellion. Government reaction to revolutionary writing was sharp and decisive. Editors and contributors were arrested, and the 'Newspaper Tax' was raised, imposing such a high duty on newspapers that their editors were forced to sell them at a price well above the reach of the poor.

But, as is always the case, while repression grew harsher, 'underground' radicalism grew stronger and more determined. Clandestine rebellion reached a destructive peak during the famous 'Luddite' outbursts of 1811 and 1812. The Luddites were small bands of desperate and daring men who travelled around the country breaking into factories and destroying machinery. Claiming to be led by a mythical figure called Ned Ludd, they had the tacit support of the workers, and their 'machine-smashing' achieved a widespread notoriety.

The war with France ended in 1815. Patriotism was no longer paramount, and rebellion came out into the open again. A series of disastrous harvests in the post-war years helped to fire discontent still further. By now, the poor had a number of determined spokesmen on their side, the most eloquent of whom was undoubtedly the journalist, William Cobbett. At its angriest and best, Cobbett's voice was a powerful one:

> Talk of *vassals*! Talk of *villains*! Talk of *serfs*! Are there any of these, or did feudal times ever see any of them, so debased, so absolutely slaves, as the poor creatures who, in the *'enlightened'* north, are *compelled* to work fourteen hours a day, in a heat of *eighty-four degrees*, and who are liable to punishment *for looking out at the window of the factory*!

Cobbett's *Political Register*, which cleverly evaded the newspaper tax by avoiding news and restricting itself to opinion, was sold at two pence a copy and had a circulation of over fifty thousand. It reached an audience far wider than its sales, though, for it was read aloud in town alehouses and country inns, where crowds gathered to hear its editor's impassioned pronouncements. The same crowds listened to new journals which followed Cobbett's lead – like Thomas Wooler's *Black Dwarf* and Richard Carlile's *Republican*. All these papers made one straightforward demand as a cure for the country's ills – the creation of a parliament that would truly represent all the people.

In August 1819, sixty thousand people congregated in St Peter's Fields, Manchester, to hear the most popular radical speaker of the day, Henry Hunt, make a speech on the subject of parliamentary reform. Under the orders of the local magistrates, the Manchester militia charged and fired upon the crowd, killing eleven people and injuring several hundred more. The 'Peterloo Massacre' as it came to be known, caused an immediate feeling of revulsion at all levels of society (see plate 17). Undeterred, the government passed its most repressive measures yet – the infamous 'Six Acts', which, amongst other things, empowered magistrates to search homes, break up meetings, and convict offenders without trial. They also extended the range of the newspaper tax to cover *all* periodicals, regardless of whether they contained news or not.

Britain certainly seemed to be on the verge of violent revolution in 1820, but fate had a hand in preventing it. Trade was good, and harvests were good. There was a sudden atmosphere of tranquillity from about 1821 onwards, and the government

17. The greatest cartoonist of his day, George Cruikshank, attacks the Peterloo Massacre.

calmed down. The Combination Acts were repealed, allowing the workers to form legal trades unions. When trade slumped in 1826, there was a countrywide outburst of strikes. But the government was no longer in the mood for repression. At last it seemed to have learnt its lesson, by realizing that the more repressive it was, the more it would provoke the desire for rebellion.

By 1830, the Tory party had enjoyed rule as the governing party for almost two generations. Largely because of the savage measures of the 1790s and the years after the war, the Tories were regarded as men of unflinching reaction – men from whom, as long as they remained in power, there could be no hope of parliamentary reform. So naturally when the opposition party, the Whigs, were swept into government in 1830, the poor and their radical leaders sensed the arrival of better times. They were right to feel this in a way, but their struggle was still to be a long one. When reform at last arrived, the government which approved it was still deeply opposed to the idea of giving the vote to *everybody*. In fact the Great Reform Bill of 1832 only extended the franchise to another 217,000 voters – a less than fifty per cent increase on the half-million landowners who had previously been allowed to vote. Out of a population which had now reached fifteen million, less than a million had the right to choose their government.

Who were these new voters? A radical journal, *The Poor Man's Guardian*, bitterly answered that question:

> The promoters of the Reform Bill projected it, not with a view to subvert, or even remodel our aristocratic institutions, but to consolidate them by a reinforcement of sub-aristocracy from the middle-classes.

In a sense, the Reform Bill was a gesture of gratitude to the men whose untiring application and enterprise had created the country's wealth and industrial prosperity – the 'new men', the 'sub-aristocracy' of moneyed manufacturers. Thousands of poor men and women had demonstrated in favour of parliamentary reform, and they now saw the vote being given to those whom they held to be responsible for their discontent. They had been betrayed, and they knew it. Agitation continued, spread, and became stronger, culminating in the Chartist movement of the late 1830s and 1840s (see plate 18). Chartism took its name from the famous 'People's Charter', drawn up by two radicals, William Lovett and Francis Place. Among its demands, the charter called for universal suffrage – or one man, one vote – secret ballots, annual parliaments, and the payment of MPs. Chartism began as a peaceful and organized movement, but it was to become more violently angry as the years passed, largely through the influence of a fiery Irishman called Feargus O'Connor, who believed that the new world could only be achieved by bloody revolution.

In the 1840s, conditions for the great majority of people were worse than they had ever been. Nearly half of the British population, which was now in the region of twenty million, were town-dwellers, and it is an indisputable fact that the manufacturing towns of Britain in the middle of the nineteenth century were disgusting places in which to have to live (see plate 19). The reports

18. A Chartist demonstration in London in the 1840s.

of various parliamentary committees, set up during the course of the century to inquire into the state of the towns, serve to remind us of this horror. In 1843, a report on Sheffield read as follows:

> Sheffield is one of the dirtiest and most smoky towns I ever saw. . . . The town is also very hilly, and the smoke ascends the streets, instead of leaving them. . . . One cannot be long in the town without experiencing the necessary inhalation of soot, which accumulates in the lungs . . .

Overcrowding was also a problem, and was often accompanied by a ghastly lack of sanitation. In Birmingham 'the privies in the old courts are in a most filthy condition . . . without doors and overflowing with filth.' In the streets of Bradford 'pools of slop water and filth are visible all over the surface.' In a particular section of Manchester 'there is only one privy for 380 inhabitants, which is placed in a narrow passage, whence its effluvia infest the adjacent houses.' It is hardly surprising that disease was rampant in such confined, deathly conditions. Cholera was a permanent threat. In 1849, a letter appeared in *The Times*, accompanied by fifty-four signatures:

> May we beg and beseech your proteckshion and power. We are, Sur, as it may be, living in a Wilderniss, so far as the rest of London knows anything of us, or as the rich and the great people care about. We live in muck and filth. We aint got no *privez*, dust bins, no drains, no water splies, and no drain or suer in the whole place. . . . The stenche of a gully-hole is disgustin. We al of us suffur, and numbers are ill, and if the colera comes Lord help us . . .

'Every day that I live,' wrote an American at about this time, 'I thank Heaven that I am not a poor man with a family in England.' Another foreigner to be deeply shocked was the German Frederick Engels, whose father set up a cotton mill in Manchester in 1842. Three years later, Engels' book *The Condition of the Working Class in England* was published in Germany. Along with works like *Das Kapital* (which Karl Marx began to compose in the reading-room of the British Museum in the 1850s) it was a book that was to have a profound effect on European social and political thought, for, apart from being an impassioned, detailed and highly readable account of the state of the English working-class in the 1840s, it bore the seeds of a revolutionary philosophy called communism – a philosophy which was to come to startling fruition in the Russian Revolution of 1917.

With frightening conviction, Engels wrote of

> the deep wrath of the whole working-class from Glasgow to London . . . a wrath which before too long . . . must break out into a Revolution in comparison with which the French Revolution . . . will prove to have been child's play.

But the terrible revolution never came. This was despite the fact that the rest of Europe was thrown into a frenzy of violent rebellion in 1848. In Britain, the most important political event of that year was the collapse of the Chartist movement, which occurred largely because of O'Connor's strident calls for a bloody overthrow of the government. Most British people, it seemed, did not want a revolution.

19. Photography's dawn captures the squalor of a Glasgow slum.
This picture was taken in the 1860s.

To a certain extent, this was because, despite the terrible conditions that had to be endured by the working-class, there were already a few clear signs that something was being done to improve these conditions. Certain philanthropic individuals will always be remembered for their energetic efforts to solve the problems created by the Industrial Revolution while those problems were still being born. One of these was Edwin Chadwick, who was responsible for two vital pieces of legislation. The first – the Poor Law Amendment Act – prevented employers from paying their workers starvation-wages on the assumption that the parish authorities, who were theoretically responsible for ensuring that nobody in a parish starved, would supplement these wages with extra money or goods. Under the new law, relief of this kind was abolished, and those who could not find work and wished to survive had to enter a parish 'workhouse', where they would be given food and a bed in return for various community chores. Unfortunately, the new system was as flagrantly abused as the old one – several workhouses were ghastly places which imposed a harsh discipline on their inmates – but Chadwick can hardly be blamed for the way in which less charitable people twisted an idea that had emerged from a sincere concern for the plight of the poor. Chadwick's second piece of legislation – the Public Health Act – set up a Board of Health and ensured the establishment of local boards throughout the country. It was more immediately successful, and certainly more popular.

Another man who cared, and cared deeply, was Lord Ashley, later Earl of Shaftesbury. His concern was for women and children. By 1850, as a result of his untiring appeals to parliament, manufacturers were prevented from employing children under the age of nine, and had to restrict the working hours of women and children to ten a day. Mine owners could no longer employ women, girls, or boys under the age of ten. Inspectors were appointed to ensure that these rules were obeyed. By our standards, conditions were still harsh, but they were infinitely better than they had been in the cruel chaos of twenty years before.

No account of the Industrial Revolution can omit the name of

Robert Owen, if only to emphasise the fact that not all employers were as cruel as history has often painted them. Owen was a cotton manufacturer who, along with several other mill owners, set up a 'model' industrial community at New Lanark in Scotland. He paid his workers well, gave them good lodgings, provided their children with a free education, and never overworked anybody. What so impressed his contemporaries, and made New Lanark something of a place of pilgrimage, was the fact that he did all this and *still* made a profit. In later life, he became too much of a dreamer, filling his head with over-idealistic schemes, such as the formation of the Grand National Consolidated Trades Union, which was the first attempt in British history to create a fully organized trades union movement. The project collapsed in 1834, but the memory of Owen's ideas and efforts lived on as proof that a society did not have to be grasping and competitive in order to be prosperous. He has justly been called the father of British socialism.

Chadwick, Ashley and Owen undoubtedly had a hand in preventing that fearful revolution which Engels predicted. So, without question, did the Reform Bill. In spite of its minimal effect on the size of the franchise, it had proved something very important. It had shown that the old world could be superseded gently and without bloodshed – in an evolutionary rather than a revolutionary way. And from 1832 onwards, more and more people began to realize that further reforms were not only possible but inevitable. No amount of stubbornness on the part of successive governments could now halt society's advance towards a complete and genuine democracy.

The Bill was important in another respect. Through a generous redistribution of seats, the large industrial towns were given parliamentary representation for the first time. Perhaps more significantly, several old rural seats were abolished. Many of these rural seats now had tiny populations and an even tinier number of voters. Some had no voters at all, and yet they still returned two members to parliament whenever there was a general election. The abolition of these 'rotten boroughs', as they were called, was a highly symbolic move. It was a sort of death-blow to the rural aristocracy, and it marked the end of that static traditional world which they had dominated for so long.

In Elizabeth Gaskell's novel *North and South*, published in 1854, John Thornton, a manufacturer no doubt very proud of his ability to vote, explains why he prefers the bustling atmosphere of a northern industrial town to what still seemed to be the quieter more traditional air of the South:

> I won't deny that I am proud of belonging to a town . . . I would rather be a man toiling, suffering – nay, failing and successless – here, than lead a dull prosperous life in the old worn grooves of what you call more aristocratic society down in the South . . . It is one of the great beauties of our system, that a working-man may raise himself into the power and position of a master by his own exertion . . .

The argument may run that it is all right for John Thornton, sitting in the comfort of his big house overlooking the factory, to express such a conviction. But there is nonetheless a truth in what he says. This thriving urban society was the new world. It was a world of appalling suffering and squalor, of course, but it was also a world of unprecedented opportunity, characterized by new thoughts, new feelings, and a new sort of freedom. Nobody was any longer claiming that the misery and deprivation were in some way pre-ordained and unalterable, and that any one section of society had any more of a God-given right to enjoy wealth and power than any other. *Nothing* was pre-ordained or unalterable or God-given. Everything was possible.

꘎꘎꘎꘎꘎

# THE ROMANTICS

꘎꘎꘎꘎꘎

## I. AN EXCITED DAWN

ALL the things we associate with the Romantics are the things we associate with being young – passionate love, egotism, lack of respect for authority, hatred of discipline, unbridled feeling, frustration, a spirit of inquiry and an enthusiasm for the new. Conversely the attributes of Augustanism are those we accord to maturity and old age – reasoned and careful argument, a belief in order and discipline, a distrust of excess, and a quiet contentment with things as they are. Romanticism in literature and art, which overthrew the Augustan classical values of the eighteenth century, was a rebellion of the young against the old.

> Bliss was it in that dawn to be alive
> But to be young was very heaven!

That was how William Wordsworth (see plate 20) looked back on the days of his youth. He was in his thirties when he wrote those lines, the nineteenth century had begun, and he was recalling the early years of the French Revolution, years in which he, along with so many others, had sensed with excitement that they were witnessing the dawn of a new world.

The critic William Hazlitt was to say of that dawn's effect on literature:

> The change in belles-lettres was as complete, and to many persons as startling, as the change in politics, with which it went hand in hand.

It must indeed have seemed a startling change. Imagine having

20. William Wordsworth in 1798, the year of the *Lyrical Ballads*.

been brought up in the glittering socially secure world of the eighteenth century, nursed on rhyme, reason and good sense, opening a book called *Lyrical Ballads*, and coming, quite suddenly and for the first time, upon deeply personal, haunting lines like these:

Five years have passed; five summers, with the length
Of five long winters! and again I hear
These waters, rolling from their mountain-springs
With a soft inland murmur — Once again
Do I behold these steep and lofty cliffs,
That on a wild secluded scene impress
Thoughts of more deep seclusion . . .

More than mildly dismayed, you turn the pages in a strange disbelief. You are to be shocked still further. You read this:

The very deep did rot: Oh Christ!
That ever this should be!
Yea, slimy things did crawl with legs
Upon the slimy sea.

The first passage is from *Tintern Abbey*, by Wordsworth, the second from *The Ancient Mariner*, by Samuel Taylor Coleridge. The *Lyrical Ballads*, first published in 1798, was a collection of poems by both men. In many ways, Wordsworth's approach to poetry was very different from that of his friend Coleridge. But the two young poets were united in one respect. They wanted to break completely with the past, by writing verse that was uncompromisingly personal and, above all, deeply felt. Only by doing this, could they give poetry the wide appeal that they sincerely believed it ought to have. In his preface to the *Ballads*, Wordsworth wrote that they wished to produce 'a class of poetry . . . well adapted to interest mankind personally', by which he meant *all* mankind, irrespective of class or education. He spoke of a new language, which was essentially the language of the heart. 'Such a language,' he wrote,

arising out of repeated experience and regular feelings, is a more permanent, and a far more philosophical language, than that which is frequently substituted for it by Poets, who think that they are conferring honour upon themselves and their art, in proportion as they separate themselves from the sympathies of men . . .

The *Lyrical Ballads* met with a confused and largely hostile reaction when they were first published. But at least William Hazlitt, on listening to Coleridge read him a selection from the book, recognized something new and refreshing:

> the sense of a new style and a new spirit in poetry came over me. It
> had to me something of the effect that arises from the turning up of
> the fresh soil, or of the first welcome breath of spring . . .

He knew that this was the Romantic rebellion, and that literature
would never be the same again.

But it was not a revolution that sprang up out of the soil one
morning in the late eighteenth century completely without warning. We have already seen how, in the 1740s, the first English
novelists had written about natural feelings in natural situations
so as to appeal to a wider and less aristocratic readership. But we
must go back further in time, and into the exclusive world of the
gentry, if we wish to find the source of Romanticism. It was a
gentleman, the Earl of Shaftesbury, who wrote as early as 1709:

> I shall no longer resist the passion growing in me for things of a
> *natural* kind; where neither *art*, nor the conceit or caprice of man, has
> spoiled their genuine order, by breaking in upon that *primitive state*.

Shaftesbury was talking about gardens, or what we should now
call 'grounds' – the huge estates that surrounded the country
houses of Britain. His views reflected a move away from the
mathematically organized gardens of the sixteenth and seventeenth centuries, and a growing taste for greater informality, a
desire to make the grounds look more like an untouched, natural
landscape (see plate 21).

This taste also extended to a fascination for the more 'natural'
and 'primitive' works of man himself – particularly for the ruined
churches and monasteries that littered the countryside. The
gentry saw these ruins as relics of a dark past about which they
knew very little, and they were thrilled by their gloomy mystery.
They were called 'Gothic', because they were assumed to have
been built, not by learned and enlightened monks, but by men
who were little more than barbarians – the 'Goths', who, it was
thought, had poured down from the wild north to destroy classical
civilization, and who, as the diarist John Evelyn had written,
'having demolished the Greek and Roman architecture, intro-

21. A sixteenth century house in an informal eighteenth-century setting. The house is Longleat in Wiltshire, the grounds were designed by the greatest of all landscape-gardeners, Lancelot 'Capability' Brown.

duced a certain fantastical and licentious manner of building which we have since called . . . Gothic.'

If a gentleman was not fortunate enough to possess a genuine ruin in his grounds, he would build one. These 'sham-ruins', or 'follies', were often made of ephemeral materials such as plaster or canvas, materials which emphasized their playfully artificial and theatrical nature. They were not things to be taken too seriously. The dark forces they symbolized were not yet strong enough to threaten the calm self-confidence of the men who built them. Neither for that matter was the 'natural' quality of the grounds in which they stood. Although the view from a country house may have looked like untamed nature, it was not untamed, but nature groomed and controlled by man.

The Augustan world moved a step further towards Romanticism when, in 1750, Horace Walpole built himself 'a little Gothick castle' at Strawberry Hill, just outside London (see plate 22). To us, this delightful building seems hardly less playful than the average sham-ruin. It is a quite fantastic thing of turrets and battlements and spires and pointed windows. But the important thing about it was that it was not a garden-ornament, but a home, a place in which Walpole elected to live. He was breathing the spirit of Gothic in his daily life, not simply looking at it from a safe distance.

From 1750 onwards, interest in the Gothic became increas-

22. Horace Walpole's 'Gothick castle', Strawberry Hill.

ingly serious and scholarly, and it went beyond architecture to embrace the written word. Collections of ballads, songs and romances, salvaged from the distant and mysterious past, were published – some of them genuine, like Thomas Percy's *Reliques of Ancient English Poetry*, others mere fabrications, like James Macpherson's infamous 'translations' of Gaelic poetry, or the work of the ill-fated genius, Thomas Chatterton, who died in 1770 when he was only eighteen. The primitivism and 'natural' vigour of these collections, which were very popular, helped to undermine the educated formality of the classical tradition in literature.

They also had a considerable influence on the work of Scotland's greatest writer, Sir Walter Scott, who published his own collection of old ballads, *The Minstrelsy of the Scottish Border*, in 1802. Scott's original verse was consciously medieval in theme and tone, and several of his novels (it was as a highly prolific novelist that he earned a renown surpassing that of any of his literary contemporaries) were set against a highly colourful and well-researched medieval background.

Another challenge to the classical tradition came from a literary fashion that was altogether less earnestly truthful in its evocation of the past – the craze for Gothic 'horror' novels. The first of these – *The Castle of Otranto* – was by Horace Walpole, and it was published in 1767. Inspired by a dream Walpole claimed to have had at Strawberry Hill – 'a very natural dream for a head filled like mine with Gothic story' – it was a tale of ghostly vengeance set in the dim world of the thirteenth century, and was an instant success. Walpole's friend, the poet Thomas Gray, wrote that it made 'some of us cry a little, and all in general afraid to go to bed o' nights', which was exactly the effect Walpole wished it to have. He wanted to appeal to his readers' feelings rather than their thoughts, and, by striking fear into their hearts, terrify them, quite literally, *out of their wits*. He did this by entering the half-lit realm of dreams and visions, a realm in which what he called 'cold reason' held no sway. Significantly, he claimed to have written the book in one long sitting and in a very 'unreasonable' fashion:

> I gave reign to my imagination; visions and passions choked me. I wrote in spite of critics, and philosophers; it seems to me the better for that.

This was a sort of eighteenth century version of what we might call 'writing off the top of one's head', and altogether a very un-Augustan way of producing literature.

Someone who wrote in even greater defiance of 'rules, critics and philosophers' was the unique novelist Laurence Sterne. His *Life and Opinions of Tristram Shandy* – issued in parts between 1760 and 1767 – does not have an immediately recognizable plot, it jumps, jolts, digresses, breaking off in mid-chapter or even in mid-sentence to career off in a variety of seemingly un-related directions. But it is still tantalizingly readable, and it had a purpose. Sterne's intention was to take his readers on a sort of drunken journey through his own mind. 'Tis', he wrote, 'a picture of myself.' In presenting the mind *as it really was* – a complex tangle of feelings, prejudices, suggestions and half-thoughts – Sterne could claim with some justice that he was being far more 'natural' than those who had been writing accord-ing to the rules of reason, logic and proportion.

In France, the philosopher Jean-Jacques Rousseau was baring, not only his mind, but his soul too, to an astonished world. He wrote in the introduction to his *Confessions*:

> I wish to reveal to my fellow-men a man completely true to nature; and that man will be myself. Myself alone. I know my heart and . . . I am unlike any other person I have seen . . . If I am not better, at least I am different.

That was bold intention in the days when Rousseau expressed it. But he was a man who believed deeply in the sanctity of a person's individuality. It was something to be cherished and nurtured, not suppressed by regulations and codes of behaviour.

He also held the view that man was born virtuous and free, with an instinctive ability to distinguish right from wrong, and that the world's evil and misery, far from being pre-destined and inevitable, were the direct result of the corruption by society of this natural state of goodness. The best men, he said, were the ones who were least tainted by contact with society, those who lived the simple life, far from wealth and cities and 'culture', and in close harmony with nature.

Rousseau's views, which extended into the fields of education and politics, inspired the begetters of the French Revolution. But they were profoundly influential in the rest of Europe, too. In England they were read by many an enlightened gentleman as he sat or reclined in the 'natural' beauty of his grounds (see plate 23). They were also the intellectual basis for Wordsworth's poetry.

But the themes and the style of English poetry began to change before Rousseau's influence was felt. James Thomson's *The Seasons*, published between 1726 and 1730, was a monumental hymn to nature, describing the simple beauty of natural things and the feelings of tenderness and sympathy that such things provoked in the observer. And in 1750 Thomas Gray published his *Elegy Written in a Country Church Yard*, a work whose plain sedate style was very different from the witty elegance of Augustan poetry. The subject of the poem was not Augustan either. Led

23. *Sir Brooke Boothby*, by Joseph Wright of Derby. Reclining romantically, he is reading Rousseau.

into solitary contemplation by the landscape and the approach of night, the poet wonders about the people buried in the church-yard in which he sits – they are simple country people, un-mourned except by the local few. But in Gray's opinion they are not unworthy of celebration:

> Let not ambition mock their useful toil,
> Their homely joys, and destiny obscure;
> Nor grandeur hear with a disdainful smile,
> The short and simple annals of the poor.

Poetry was moving out of its courtly, literate setting and into the countryside, where life seemed purer, happier, and more honest.

The finest contemplative nature poet before the rise of Words-worth was unquestionably William Cowper, whose first works were published in 1779. Cowper's sincere and easeful tributes to nature and the rural life made everything that preceded them – including Gray's *Elegy* – seem slightly mannered and self-conscious:

> Here Ouse, slow winding through the level plain
> Of spacious meads with cattle sprinkled o'er,
> Conducts the eye along its sinuous course
> Delighted . . .
> While far beyond, and overthwart the stream
> That, as with molten glass, inlays the vale,
> The sloping land recedes into the clouds . . .

While Cowper was writing, an even more 'genuine' and spon-taneous voice was emerging from Scotland:

> Gie me ae spark o' Nature's fire,
> That's a' the learning I desire;
> Then, tho' I drudge thro' drub an' mire
>     At pleugh or cart,
> My Muse, tho' hamely in attire,
>     May touch the heart.

This was the brittle and unique voice of Robert Burns. He was the son of a farmer, and his purpose was to capture the spirit and the language of the poor country-people of Scotland. He produced hundreds of songs, lyrics and ballads, ranging from the hauntingly beautiful to the savagely comic – all of them tautly direct and simple in tone.

A poet with a far bleaker view of nature than either Cowper or Burns was George Crabbe. His most celebrated poem, *The Village*, published in 1783, was written as a brutally honest corrective to Goldsmith's *The Deserted Village*. In his anger at the advance of enclosure, Goldsmith had depicted village life as an enviable round of uninterrupted bliss. Crabbe's concern was to tell the truth, by which he meant the *real truth*, which was hardly blissful:

> No longer truth, though shown in verse, disdain,
> But own the Village Life a life of pain.

Lord Byron was to refer to Crabbe as 'Nature's sternest painter'. Here is an example which proves the truth of that description:

> Rank weeds, that every art and care defy,
> Reign o'er the land, and rob the blighted rye:
> There thistles stretch their prickly arms afar,
> And to the ragged infant threaten war;
> There poppies nodding, mock the hope of toil;
> There the blue bugloss paints the sterile soil . . .

Nature, in Crabbe's view, was no longer to be regarded as the countryman's warm companion. Neither was she an obedient one. She had a capricious independence, a wild life of her own, defying control.

The Augustans had thought of nature as a plaything, a beautiful toy, created by God for man's enjoyment, incapable of threatening man's supremacy in the Scale of Being. But now she had taken on a new, powerful role – the dominant one in that relationship. She had become something that could not, and should not, be controlled by man, for she was greater than man, a strong, dark, indefinable force that man could not begin to comprehend. Wordsworth sensed this mysterious power when he was only a boy. In his autobiographical poem *The Prelude*, he recalled how, on a summer evening in his childhood, he had taken a boat out on to the lake near his home in the Lake District:

I dipped my oars into the silent lake,
And, as I rose upon the stroke, my boat
Went heaving through the water like a swan;
When, from behind that craggy steep till then
The horizon's bound, a huge peak, black and huge,
As if with voluntary power instinct
Upreared its head. I struck and struck again,
And growing still in stature the grim shape
Towered up between me and the stars, and still,
For so it seemed, with purpose of its own
And measured motion like a living thing,
Strode after me.

He was both frightened and thrilled. His terror had made him discover what he called 'unknown modes of being . . . huge and mighty forms' – in other words, the *living power* of the great goddess Nature, before whom man, in his new weakness, must tremble in awe and worship. At that decisive moment, Wordsworth realized that he must dedicate his life and work to her. The concern of his poetry, he wrote, was

Not with the mean and vulgar works of man,
But with high objects, with enduring things –

That was as fine a statement of Romanticism's purpose as any.

Amongst painters, there was a similar shift of emphasis. Until 1750, the predominant taste in painting was for faces – a taste which subscribed to Pope's Augustan dictum

The proper study of mankind is man.

But Thomas Gainsborough, in an honest moment, confessed that he was 'sick of Portraits', and that his real desire was to 'walk off to some sweet village where I can paint landskips.' He let nature creep into the background of his portraits, and, occasionally, he would allow his true passion to reign supreme.

From 1750 onwards, less celebrated painters devoted themselves exclusively to painting landscapes. Out of this interest emerged what is often considered to be the only truly unique British contribution to painting in general – the watercolour.

The most brilliant of the English watercolourists was Thomas Girtin, who died when he was only twenty-seven years old in 1802. Girtin was concerned with strict accuracy. He painted what he saw. Because he had a fine eye for light and atmosphere, his art was radiantly personal, but it was nonetheless based on the landscape as it existed (see plate 24). 'Had Girtin lived,' said Turner, 'I should have starved.' As a young man, Turner worked closely with Girtin, and he was deeply influenced by his colleague's emphasis on realism. Turner is better known for the uniquely cataclysmic paintings of his later life, so he strictly belongs to the second section of this chapter. But an early painting like *Buttermere Lake* – *not* a watercolour incidentally – seems to capture the essence of Wordsworthian Romanticism (see plate 25). First exhibited in 1798 – the year of the *Lyrical Ballads* – it is a perfect realization of the haunting lakeland landscape which inspired the great poet.

But the real Wordsworth of painting – and the greatest of all the British landscape-painters – was John Constable. Constable wrote:

> I was born to paint . . . my own dear old England; and when I cease to love her, may I, as Wordsworth says, 'never more hear her green leaves rustle, and her torrents roar'.

Constable's letters and notebooks are filled with gentle Wordsworthian pronouncements on nature and art. He was a true Romantic in that he rejected learning and academic precedent. Wordsworth wrote:

> Up! Up! my friend, and quit your books . . .
> Let nature be your teacher.

Constable obeyed that instruction. He said that whenever he settled down to start on a sketch, 'the first thing I try to do is, *to forget that I have ever seen a picture.*' How different such an approach was to that of the great 'classical' painter, Sir Joshua Reynolds, whose primary instruction to the students of the Royal Academy had been to 'study the great masters', and who also said: 'A mere copier of nature can never produce anything great.'

24. Thomas Girtin's *Kirkstall Abbey*: a superb watercolour with a clearly Romantic theme.

25. Turner's *Buttermere Lake*.

Like Wordsworth, Constable had a sort of personal relationship – almost a love-affair – with nature, in which feeling was the keynote. 'Painting with me is but another word for feeling', he said. There were certain aspects of the Wordsworthian temperament, however, which Constable did not share. When he visited the Lake District in 1806, in order to sketch the landscape that was already famous for its effect on Wordsworth, he found it depressing. He wrote: 'The solitude of mountains oppresses my spirit.' He preferred the simpler, quieter beauties of the East Anglian landscape into which he had been born and from which he never liked to stray for too long (see colour plate 4).

But his sharp eye would have delighted in the smaller details of nature that so pleased Wordsworth's sister Dorothy, whose journal entries were often used as a basis for her brother's gentler lyrics. Here is her description of the arrival of spring in the orchard at Grasmere:

There is yet one primrose in the orchard. The stitchwort is fading.
The wild columbines are coming into beauty. The vetches are in
abundance, Blossoming and seeding. That pretty little waxy-looking
Dial-like yellow flower, the speedwell, and some others whose names
I do not yet know . . .

Two days after this entry, Dorothy Wordsworth, not content
with half-knowledge, identified the 'yellow flower' as 'Lysi-
machia Nemorum, Yellow Pimpernell of the Woods'. We can
assume, too, that she was not slow to find out the names of the
other plants she could not identify at the time of writing. For she
combined a deep love of nature with that determined spirit of
inquiry which characterized the age in which she lived.

In the early days of Romanticism, science and the imagination
worked hand in hand. It was not enough to gaze in awe at the
mysteries of nature – it was important to study them too. Typi-
cally, Constable wrote: 'Painting is a science, and should be
pursued as an enquiry into the laws of nature.' But it was also
'another word for feeling'. Perhaps the best description of
Constable's work is that of a modern art-historian, Kenneth
Clark, who calls it a 'romantic combination of science and
ecstasy'.

That combination is at once evident in a picture called
*Experiment on a Bird in the Air-Pump*, painted in 1768 by Joseph
Wright of Derby (see plate 26). Like Constable, Wright regarded
his work as a form of scientific experimentation, and he was
especially interested in the effects of light and shadow on the
human face. The painting clearly demonstrates this interest. It
also has an obviously scientific theme. But the situation depicted
is nonetheless informed by deep feeling. Helped by the strange
half-light, it is filled with a sense of wide-eyed wonder at the laws
of nature – science and ecstasy combined. Another painter who
was both romantic and scientific was George Stubbs, who was
passionately interested in anatomy, particularly in the anatomy of
the horse. This interest led him to spend four years in a lonely
Lincolnshire farmhouse, dissecting horse-carcasses, and drawing
what he found. Many of his horse-paintings have a cool, classical
austerity, but his more personal paintings reflect a new taste for
the wild and the mysterious (see plate 27).

26. Joseph Wright's *Experiment on a Bird in the Air-Pump.*

27. A Romantic Stubbs: *Horse Devoured by a Lion.*

Stubbs' work in anatomy earned him the respect of the most eminent scientists of his day, while the industrialists of the age, interested in inquiries and innovations of all kinds, were not slow to express their appreciation. Stubbs' best known patron was the potter Josiah Wedgwood, who employed him to produce decorations for his pottery. Joseph Wright also enjoyed Wedgwood's patronage, as well as that of the scientist and philosopher Joseph Priestley, and the cotton-manufacturer Richard Arkwright.

Another man of the imagination who enjoyed the friendship of scientists and industrialists was the poet Erasmus Darwin, a man of considerable literary stature in his time, much respected by Wordsworth amongst others. Together with men like Wedgwood, Priestley and James Watt, he was a co-founder of the Birmingham Lunar Society, which met once a month on the Monday nearest the full moon. At these meetings, talk about the latest discoveries and inventions was liberally sprinkled with observations on philosophy, art and literature. In such a distinguished and cultured company, Darwin naturally perceived a beneficial co-operation between science and the arts. It was to promote this co-operation that he wrote his poem *The Botanic Garden*, published in 1792. The most famous lines from the poem are those in which Darwin excitedly describes the infinite potential of steam-power:

> Soon shall thy arm, UNCONQUER'D STEAM! afar
> Drag the slow barge, or drive the rapid car;
> Or on wide-waving wings expanded bear
> The flying-chariot through the fields of air.

The dawn of Romanticism and the dawn of industrialization were simultaneous, and to begin with there was very little feeling that the arts and the sciences were in any way opposed to each other. To most men of culture and intellect, the spirit of inquiry and innovation was not a threat, but rather something that was worthy of excited admiration, and in which they were eager to participate. Philosophers, artists, writers, scientists, inventors and manufacturers were working together to undermine the rigid structure of the old world.

But whose is this biblical, doom-laden voice?

> . . . all the arts of life they chang'd into the
>   arts of death . . .
> And in their stead intricate wheels invented,
>   Wheel without wheel,
> To perplex youth in their outgoings & to bind
>   to labours in Albion
> Of day & night the myriads of eternity . . .
>      . . . that they might spend
>   the days of wisdom
> In sorrowful drudgery.

It is a vision of industry, but it lacks any sense of excitement or hope. It is the picture of an earthly hell, written by the poet and artist William Blake. He wrote the lines in 1794, when most writers and artists were still excited by the dawning of a new age. The full shock of disillusionment had not yet arrived. But Blake already knew the true horror of what was happening. The spirit of discovery – the march of progress – was not only forcing more and more people into urban poverty, but it was killing individuality, stifling life's essence, by turning men into brutes – worse still, into machines. Blake never had any faith in the powers of science. To him, they were 'the arts of death'.

Blake was a man who wrote before his time, a true prophet. So he belongs to Romanticism's second stage – characterized by an essentially sad, visionary inwardness.


II. SINKINGS AND MISGIVINGS

Most early Romantics had found the real world sufficiently exciting in itself to feed their imaginations. The later Romantics found the real world depressingly ugly and cruel, and so they turned in on themselves, searching their minds for a world that would assure them of the existence of greater, more permanent truths – the truths of love and deep feeling and beauty.

They were fascinated by dreams and visions. It was a dream of a hand in armour on the staircase of Strawberry Hill that inspired *The Castle of Otranto*. But Horace Walpole was too firmly rooted in the eighteenth-century distrust of the irrational to consider his dream, and his book, as anything more than a diverting departure from the real world. The true Romantics took dreams far more seriously. They represented what Shelley called 'gleams of a remoter world'.

The 'Gothic' horror novels that followed in the wake of Walpole's book – novels like Anne Radcliffe's *The Mysteries of Udolpho*, or Matthew Lewis's *The Monk* – had to a certain extent opened the doors into this 'remoter world'. In painting, the way had been paved by a strange Swiss-born painter called Henry Fuseli, who first arrived in England in 1764. He rapidly made a name for himself as a painter of fantastic visionary scenes which sent strange thrills of discomfort down the spines of the Royal Academy's fashionable visitors (see plate 28). Fuseli was unlike his contemporaries in that he did not have the slightest interest in nature or in landscape. His eye was essentially inward-looking. Dreams and visions were his landscape – the real world was not.

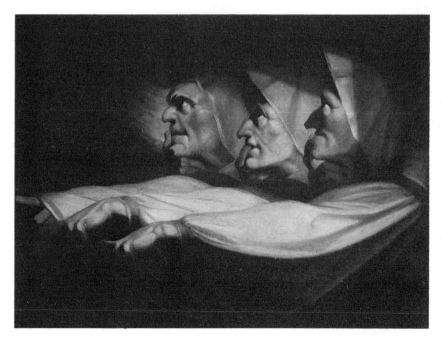

28. *The Three Witches* by Henry Fuseli.

The young William Blake worked as an engraver for Fuseli, and no true genius has been more consistently inward-looking than Blake, who was both an artist and a poet (see colour plate 5). 'Imagination is My World,' he wrote, 'this world of Dross is beneath my notice.' Landscape painting reminded him of 'the world of vegetation', and he found 'drawing from life . . . hateful because it suggested 'death' and 'mortality', and his concern was with 'the world of Eternity', which he believed to be synonymous with the world of the imagination. 'Vision of Imagination,' he wrote, 'is a representation of what Eternally Exists, Really and Unchangeably.'

Blake was a true visionary – he experienced, as far as we can tell, absolutely genuine visions. At a very young age, he apparently saw, while fully conscious, God at his bedroom window, and he also claimed to have once encountered the prophet Ezekiel sitting under a tree. This power to experience hallucinations that were as real to him as the natural world never left him. So perhaps he really saw what he described in this strange little lyric:

> The fields from Islington to Marybone,
> To primrose Hill and Saint John's Wood,
> Were builded over with pillars of gold,
> And there Jerusalem's pillars stood.

He echoed this lyric in the famous poem – now better known as a hymn – which ends with the lines:

> I will not cease from Mental Fight,
> Nor shall my Sword sleep in my hand,
> Till we have built Jerusalem,
> In England's green & pleasant Land.

When Blake spoke of Jerusalem he was not simply referring to the Holy City that is the centre of the Christian faith. To him, it was something far less specific – a paradise of the imagination, informed by joy, spontaneity, genius and beauty.

Despite his sense of separation from the world, Blake was a very happy man. The painter Samuel Palmer wrote: 'If asked whether I ever knew, among the intellectual, a happy man, Blake

would be the only one who would immediately occur to me.' Yet
he is supposed to have said on his death-bed in 1827, according to
a friend, that 'he was going to that country he had all his life
wished to see.' Perhaps he felt that at last he was about to enter
the true Jerusalem.

Another, far less happy, Romantic who lived in a world which
bore little or no relation to the real one was William Beckford,
whose long life (1760 to 1844) spanned the age of Romanticism
more completely than that of any comparable figure. In 1786,
Beckford published a fantasy novel called *Vathek*, which was set
in an oriental dream-world, but he was not blessed with the
creative genius of his great contemporaries. However, he did
possess an awareness of the world's cruelty and a feeling of deep
isolation, sensations which were strengthened in 1784 when he
was outlawed by fashionable society for his homosexuality, which
made him a *persona non grata* for the rest of his life. Fortunately

29. Perhaps the most 'Romantic' home ever built: William Beckford's
Fonthill Abbey.

for him, he was one of the richest men in Britain, and he relieved his bitter loneliness by pouring his immense fortune into building himself an extraordinary home – Fonthill Abbey in Wiltshire. Fonthill followed the taste for medieval houses which had started with Strawberry Hill, and which, by the beginning of the nineteenth century, was becoming something of a fashionable craze. But more than any other building, Fonthill was the Romantic dream made real (see plate 29). In its dark corridors and huge halls, Beckford spent most of his time alone, living a favoured dream-life, keeping the world at bay. Its tower, which soared to a height of 276 feet, could be seen for miles, proclaiming its owner's contempt for the society which had rejected him. In 1825, the tower collapsed, as a dream collapses, and only a tiny part of the structure exists today. If it had survived, it would have been a sublime architectural monument to the Romantic spirit.

In one of his best-known poems, *Kubla Khan*, Samuel Taylor Coleridge (see plate 30) created his own inimitable dream-palace:

> In Xanadu did Kubla Khan
> A stately pleasure-dome decree:
> Where Alph, the sacred river, ran
> Through caverns measureless to man
> Down to a sunless sea.

Coleridge claimed to have composed the poem 'in a sort of reverie brought on by two grains of Opium'. It was sub-titled 'A Fragment', for it was unfinished. It ends with the expression of an anguished desire to re-enter that strange realm of which the poet has had a brief but tantalizing glimpse:

> I would build that dome in air,
> That sunny dome! those caves of ice!

Coleridge was dogged by fits of incurable despondency for much of his life. 'I suffer too often sinkings and misgivings,' he wrote, 'alienations from the spirit of hope'. His friend Wordsworth, although he was often depressed, was incapable of such deep despair. For him, the exquisite beauties of the Lake District never lost their power to comfort the mind, even in its darkest

30. Coleridge in a contemplative mood, in 1814.

moments. But Coleridge, who also lived amongst the lakes, often found little or no consolation even in the glories of nature:

> I see them all so excellently fair,
> I see, not feel, how beautiful they are!

Even as a boy, Coleridge had thought of himself as a being cut off from the rest of the world. Of his schooldays he wrote that he had already cultivated 'feelings of deep and bitter contempt for all who traversed the orbit of my understanding'. So he turned in on himself and, as he put it, he 'became a dreamer'.

Like Wordsworth, Coleridge participated with fervour in the intellectual enthusiasm for the early stages of the French Revolution. But the collapse of the revolutionary ideal and the terrible barbarity of the Reign of Terror served to remind him of something that he had experienced in the rough and tumble of the schoolyard – the awful cruelty of mankind. He realized, too, that his own country was showing signs of a cooler brutality, typified by the heartless recommendations of a man like Malthus. Malthus's views were, according to Coleridge, a perfect example of the

> accursed practice of ever considering *only* what seems *expedient* for the occasion, disjoined from all principle or . . . of ever listening to the true and unerring impulses of our better natures.

Coleridge saw himself as a champion of these 'true and unerring impulses', which were the impulses of the heart, of simple human feeling. And as he saw society being overrun by harsh expediency and cold calculation, he naturally felt alienated from the general developments of the age.

A generation of younger Romantics grew up with similar views, thinking of themselves as higher beings, separated from the rest of mankind by the intensity of their feelings and the sensitivity of their imaginations. To us, the idea of the writer or artist as a 'special' person, scribbling or sketching his individual view of the world in the loneliness of his garret, largely ignored and even rebuked by the mass of mankind, is something we accept as commonplace, but at the beginning of the nineteenth century it was a new idea, and it is a concept we owe to the Romantics. Before the Romantic age, writers and artists had regarded themselves as public servants. Theirs was a job like any other, with its duties and codes. If they were truly great, their individuality would naturally shine through, but they were always aware of the need to please those for whom they were writing, whether they were private patrons or the public as a whole. But the attitude of the Romantics to their audience was well expressed by John Keats in a letter to a friend:

> I have not the slightest feel of humility towards the public. . . . I never wrote one single Line of Poetry with the least Shadow of public thought.

Unable to respect the judgement of their public, the Romantics relied on nobody's judgement but their own. 'Everyone did that which was good in his own eyes', wrote Hazlitt. This new freedom, of course, led to some very bad work, but without it, the true geniuses of the age could not have created their masterpieces.

It would be wrong, of course, to think that the Romantics despised hard work and study, or that they shunned the works of other great minds, living or dead. They were all well-read, and their faith in their own genius did not make them spurn the idea of subjecting their work to severe self-criticism and constant revision. But ultimately, a Romantic regarded himself as his own master, however much he may have been guided by others.

Percy Bysshe Shelley (see plate 31) was undoubtedly the most arrogantly self-assured of the Romantic poets. 'Accept no counsel from the simple-minded,' he wrote, 'time reverses the judgement of the foolish crowd.' He was also the poet with the most fervent desire to escape from the world:

> I could lie down like a tired child,
> And weep away this life of care
> Which I have borne, and yet must bear,
> Till death like sleep might steal on me . . .

Death, like dreaming, was a favourite Romantic subject. It was seen as a permanent departure from mundane reality into that 'remoter world' of which dreams could only provide a brief glimpse. With Shelley, though, death was an overriding obsession, not only in his work, but in his life. He thought of killing himself more than once, and his own death, although shrouded in mystery, was unquestionably a sort of suicide. He was drowned

5. The work of a visionary: William Blake's *The Good and Evil Angels Struggling for the Possession of a Child.*

6. The Great Day of His Wrath, by John Martin

31. Shelley at the Baths of Caracalla in Rome.

off the north-east coast of Italy after deciding to brave a storm in a tiny boat. Shelley had always liked to think of the sea as a wild symbol of eternity. He continued the lines quoted above with the expression of a wish to

> hear the sea
> Breathe o'er my dying brain its last monotony.

In 1822, when he was only twenty-nine years old, his wish was granted.

Like Coleridge, Shelley thought of himself as a separate being even in his childhood. He remembered his first school as 'a perfect Hell', in which he had been bullied mercilessly, and at Eton, his strange exclusive behaviour earned him the nickname 'Mad Shelley'. At Oxford, he encountered the world's tyranny for the first time when he was expelled for publishing a pamphlet called *The Necessity of Atheism*. Unlike Coleridge, though, he interpreted his sense of being isolated and 'special' as a signal for action rather than inward contemplation. He was too young for the crippling disillusionment of the 1790s to have had any effect on him, and he was driven by a frenzied desire to convert the real world to his passionately libertarian views. He felt that the poet had a duty to use his genius in the fight against tyranny of all kinds. 'Poets,' he wrote with characteristic brashness, 'are the unacknowledged legislators of the world.'

Shelley was at the height of his powers in 1819, the year of Peterloo and the Six Acts. His view of his country in that year was a bitter one:

> An old, mad, blind, despised, and dying king, –
> Princes, the dregs of their dull race, who flow
> Through public scorn, – mud from a muddy spring . . .
> A people starved and stabbed in the untilled field . . .

But he was not despondent, for he felt that out of the misery and strife of the times

> a glorious Phantom may
> Burst, to illumine our tempestuous day.

In 1820, there were revolutions in Spain and Naples. 1821 was the year of the first Greek rising, and of revolutions in Spanish South America. The people of the world, it seemed, were at last waking up and expressing a fervent thirst for liberty, and Shelley caught the ardour of that new dawn:

> Arise, arise, arise!
> There is blood on the earth that denies ye bread;
> Be your wounds like eyes
> To weep for the dead, the dead, the dead.

He was also an unrelenting atheist, and a believer in free love. Rather too many impressionable young women suffered for his belief. He was undoubtedly a spell-binding young man – but it was a dangerous spell. One of its more tragic victims was Harriet Westbrook, who bore Shelley two children, and then, when he had left her to live with another woman, drowned herself in the Serpentine.

The other woman was Mary, the daughter of William Godwin, author of a vibrantly anarchist work called *An Enquiry concerning Political Justice*, which was published in 1793 and was regarded as something of a bible by men of libertarian beliefs – including Wordsworth, Coleridge, and, of course, Shelley himself. Mary married Shelley in 1816, and as a result of her entry into this young man's strange world, she produced one of the greatest of modern legends – *Frankenstein*, the story of a scientist who lets his passion for scientific inquiry go too far by creating a 'human' monster. Mary Shelley's depiction of the monster is an essentially sympathetic one which owes a great deal to her husband's view of himself as a man and a poet. At one point, the sad creature cries out to his creator:

> Am I not alone, miserably alone? . . . The desert mountains are my refuge. . . . The bleak skies I hail, for they are kinder to me than your fellow-beings.

In this cry, the monster, friendless and rejected, has a close affinity to the Romantic artist in his isolation and scorn for the world.

*Frankenstein* was born out of a suggestion of Lord Byron's, who in 1816 was a neighbour of the Shelleys on the shores of Lake Geneva in Switzerland, and who, when they were visiting him at his villa, had proposed that they should 'each write a ghost story' in the best Gothic tradition. Shelley's friendship with Byron was to last for the rest of his short life. When they first met in 1816, Shelley was comparatively unknown as a poet, but Byron (see plate 32), only four years older, was already a household name. In 1812, the first two cantos of his narrative poem *Childe Harold's Pilgrimage* had met with a wildly enthusiastic reception. It was the story of a 'gloomy wanderer' and his travels across Europe. The hero-narrator of the poem was a figure who seemed to speak to a generation. He was the Romantic incarnate – alone, slightly embittered, handsome, an unattached and passionate lover, searching for a companion who would teach him the meaning of true love and rid him of his fateful loneliness forever. No fashionable lady could fail to be moved by such a

32. Lord Byron.

man, and, because it was felt that Byron was painting a portrait of himself, the poet became the toast of London, entertained, and courted, by one society hostess after another. In 1816, however, he suddenly found himself outlawed for making advances to his half-sister while still officially married to an heiress, and he was forced into .exile, never to return to his native country. But although he may no longer have been acceptable as a person, his reputation as a poet was assured. The remaining three cantos of *Childe Harold*, published in 1816 and 1818, met with a reception as clamorous and delighted as that which had welcomed the first two.

Just as Shelley rather relished his solitude, so Byron enjoyed his exile. He had, after all, *become* the gloomy wanderer, scorned and alone. The lonely outcast became something of a Byronic trademark, making a notable appearance in *Manfred* – the story of a tormented fugitive, living alone amongst the Alps and obsessed by thoughts of suicide – and, finally, in Byron's true masterpiece, *Don Juan*. Dismissed from society because of a romantic intrigue, Don Juan is the most closely autobiographical of Byron's heroes. But the tone of the poem is altogether very different from the usual Romantic utterance:

> But Juan was a bachelor – of arts,
> And parts, and hearts: he danced and sung, and had
> An air as sentimental as Mozart's
> Softest of melodies; and could be sad
> Or cheerful, without any 'flaws or starts',
> Just at the proper time; and though a lad,
> Had seen the world – which is a curious sight,
> And very much unlike what people write.

This witty, slightly cynical tone relates Byron to the relaxed worldliness of the Augustans rather than to the inward-looking remorse of his contemporaries. When pressed, Byron would admit to preferring men who *did* things to those who thought and wrote and felt sorry for themselves:

> Who would write, who had any thing better to do? . . . Look at the querulous, monotonous lives of the 'genus'; . . . what a worthless, idle brood it is!

He also wrote that 'the great object of life is sensation', and his own desire to get up and be doing, to experience what he called 'keenly felt pursuits', led him to participate in the fight for freedom far more actively than Shelley ever did, firstly by making practical contributions to Italy's battle for liberation from Austrian rule, and then, in 1824, by going to Greece, which was trying to free itself from Turkish oppression. He died there in April of that year, aged thirty six, from malaria. Although Byron must have been bitterly disappointed not to have died in battle, Shelley would no doubt have envied him his death. For his name immediately reverberated throughout Europe as that of a man who had died fighting for liberty.

'It runs in my head we shall all die young,' wrote John Keats (see plate 33), a Romantic who had once confessed, like Byron, to preferring 'a life of sensations rather than thoughts'. In February 1821, three months after having made that prophesy, he died in Rome, a year and a half before Shelley, and three years before Byron, at the tragically early age of twenty-five. In his memory, Shelley wrote *Adonais*, which is not only one of Shelley's best poems, but the finest expression there is of the Romantic view of death:

> Peace, peace! he is not dead, and doth not sleep –
> He hath awakened from the dream of life –
> 'Tis we, who lost in stormy visions, keep
> With phantoms an unprofitable strife . . .

In death, Keats had soared beyond the reach of the world's cruelty:

> Envy and calumny and hate and pain . . .
> Can touch him not and torture not again;
> From the contagion of the world's slow stain
> He is secure . . .

Shelley yearned to follow him, and, a year after writing *Adonais*, he did. On his final fatal boat trip, he had a copy of Keats' poems in his pocket.

Keats himself would have found Shelley's tribute embarrassing. It is true that he often felt, like all the Romantics, alone and estranged, cut off from the rest of mankind, and that he occasionally expressed a longing for the escape provided by death:

> Now more than ever seems it rich to die,
> To cease upon the midnight with no pain . . .

But although the idea of death haunted him, he never pursued it in the way that Shelley did. In a last letter written from Naples to the mother of the girl he loved to distraction, Fanny Browne,

33. Keats in his house at Hampstead.

he wrote: 'O what an account I could give you of the Bay of Naples if I could once more feel myself a Citizen of this World.' He wrote that five months before he died. He knew he was dying.

Whereas Shelley would have relished the thought, it pained Keats, for this young man, who had once admitted to being 'half in love with easeful Death', was actually passionately in love with life, with the sheer joy of existing, of being a part of the real world.

Keats gave up a career as a surgeon to become a poet at the age of twenty-one. 'There is but one way for me,' he wrote, 'the road lies through application, study and thought'. By thought he did not mean what he called 'consequitive reasoning', but something deeper and far more immediate. He meant the sort of wisdom that comes from sensation and watchfulness, from opening our minds to all experience. 'We can judge no further but by . . . experience – for axioms in philosophy are not axioms until they are proved upon our pulses.' Keats' short life was not particularly active in the sense that Byron and Shelley's were, but because of his sharp eye and open mind, he was excited by the simplest of sensations, particularly by the rich glories of nature. It was an excitement which related him to the dawn of Romanticism, when poets and painters were perceiving, as if for the first time, the vibrancy of the natural world:

> How beautiful the season is now – How fine the air. A temperate sharpness about it . . . I never lik'd stubble fields so much as now . . .

This particular experience inspired Keats to compose his ode *To Autumn* – perhaps his greatest poem, and certainly English poetry's finest tribute to nature's plenitude:

> . . . barred clouds bloom the soft-dying day,
> And touch the stubble-plains with rosy hue;
> Then in a wailful choir the small gnats mourn
> Among the river sallows, borne aloft
> Or sinking as the light wind lives or dies . . .

The painter Samuel Palmer expressed a very Keatsian excitement at nature's richness in his notebooks:

> Nature . . . is sprinkled and showered with a thousand pretty eyes, and buds, and spires, and blossoms gemm'd with dew . . . the motley clouding; the fine meshes, the aerial tissues, that dapple the skies of spring. . . . the leafy lightness . . .

Palmer admired, and was profoundly influenced by, William Blake. But he did not share Blake's scorn for 'the world of vegetation', because he could not rely, as Blake had done, on his inward eye to inspire him. He needed the real world as his starting point. In 1827, he went to live in the secluded valley of Shoreham in Kent, and there he found a tiny portion of the real world for his purpose – a rich, bubbling abundance of nature that inspired him to produce a series of magical landscapes that are truly unique in the history of English art (see plate 34).

34. Samuel Palmer's *Early Morning*.

Palmer's paintings, like Keats' best poems, were small, meticulous gems. His style was exceptional, for the Romantic taste of the times was for the huge and the apocalyptic, a taste for paintings that would match the writing of Byron in its more turbulent moments:

> The mists boil up around the glaciers; clouds
> Rise curling fast beneath me, white and sulphury,
> Like foam from the roused ocean of deep Hell . . .

Such a taste is immediately evident in the work of John Martin, whom a contemporary described as 'a great soul lapped in majestic and unearthly dreams', and whose visions were perhaps the most extraordinary and cataclysmic ever painted (see colour plate 6).

A painter no less turbulent than Martin, but of inestimably greater genius, was Joseph Mallord William Turner. We have already seen how, as a young man, Turner painted serenely 'natural' landscapes that owed a great deal to his brilliant friend Girtin. But for all the peaceful tranquillity of these paintings – which earned him considerable fame – his true taste was for violence and catastrophe. His temperament was Byronic rather than Wordsworthian. After Girtin's death, he began to let this taste predominate, painting pictures of threatening alpine glaciers and shipwrecks at sea. His preference for the 'active' over the quietly contemplative led him to create a manner of painting that would accord with the turmoil of his subject matter – and this is how he forged the unique style that Constable called 'tinted steam', and which Hazlitt heard a fellow-critic dismiss as 'pictures of nothing'.

They were not, of course, pictures of nothing. Turner's wild and visionary washes – completely unlike anything anybody else was painting – were informed by an eye that was deeply attuned to things as they really were. For all their strangeness, the real world was their basis. One of Turner's best paintings, *Snowstorm* (see plate 35), exhibited in 1842, aroused a furore of critical abuse. One particularly angry critic called it a 'mass of soapsuds and whitewash'. Turner knew better. He had painted what he had seen, for he had been there:

> I got the sailors to lash me to the mast to observe it; I was lashed for four hours and I did not expect to escape, but I felt bound to record it if I did. But no one had any business to like it.

Proudly, he asked: 'I wonder what they think the sea's like? I wish they'd been in it.'

35. Turner's *Snowstorm*.

A true Romantic, Turner had no time for what the world thought of him or his paintings. He believed only in the power of his own genius. He also quite enjoyed his reputation as a strange, separate being lost in his own visions. In later life, he would quite deliberately leave his paintings unfinished until they had been hung in the Royal Academy, when he would rapidly complete them in public, watched by a baffled audience. Perhaps he smiled inwardly at the awed bewilderment he was creating around him.

One of the few men to understand Turner's genius and purpose at the time was John Ruskin, the greatest of the Victorian critics. In 1860, nine years after the painter's death, Ruskin paid him this exceptional but sincerely felt tribute:

> What, for us, his work yet may be, I know not. But let not the real nature of it be misunderstood any more . . . his work . . . is the loveliest ever yet done by man, in imagery of the physical world. Whatsoever is there of fairest, you will find recorded by Turner, and by Turner alone.

He followed this tribute with an observation which bemoaned the prevailing ugliness and insensitivity of his age, and which clearly demonstrates the deep sense of alienation typical of the Romantics:

> I say *you* will find, not knowing to how few I speak; for in order to find what is fairest, you must delight in what is fair; and I know not how few or how many there may be who take such delight. Once I could speak joyfully about beautiful things, thinking to be understood; – now I cannot any more; for it seems to me that no one regards them. Wherever I look or travel in England or abroad, I see that men, wherever they can reach, destroy all beauty. They seem to have no other desire or hope but to have large houses and to be able to move fast. Every perfect and lovely spot which they can touch, they defile.

These words are, of course, as true today as they were then. Perhaps they are even truer. It is because they are still true that the writers and artists of our own times have not yet been able to discard that sad mantle of loneliness bequeathed to them by their Romantic predecessors.

ᘛᘛᘛᘛᘛᘛ

# TASTE

ᘛᘛᘛᘛᘛᘛ

I T is important to remember that the age of Wordsworth, Coleridge, Keats, Shelley and Byron, was also the age of Jane Austen,
and in her world the ferment had little or no part to play. The
characters of her six brilliant novels, published between 1811 and
1818, although they are not inordinately rich, are nonetheless
wealthy enough to live virtually uninterrupted lives of leisure.
Their theatre of action is the drawing-room, the assembly-room,
the fashionable street, or the grounds of the country house. They
spend their time walking, riding, dancing, playing cards, listening to music, reading, writing letters, and, above all, conversing.
But their conversation rarely steps beyond the boundaries of their
own comfortable and closeted society. They talk about fashion
and taste, about acceptable and unacceptable behaviour, about
love, of course, and, more than anything else, about marriage.

It is an indication of Jane Austen's remarkable genius that she
managed to give this narrow world with its unimportant issues a
magical timelessness and universality. Her mastery of narrative
and her lively understanding of human behaviour could endow
the most everyday events – the arrival of a letter, the approach
of an unexpected stranger – with a significance and suspense
no less thrilling, in its own way, than the sight of a gloomy castle
or the dilemma of a Byronic hero standing on the edge of an
Alpine precipice wondering whether or not to throw himself into
the abyss.

She was not unaware of the ferment. She had two brothers who
had both seen the world as officers in the navy, and a cousin

whose husband had been guillotined during the French Revolution. She read Wordsworth, Coleridge, Byron, and even the republican William Godwin. But she knew instinctively that the great forces which were creating the new world were not her canvas. She recognized what she was good at and she stuck to it. She once wrote with typical modesty: 'I must keep to my own style and go on in my own way, and though I may never succeed again in that, I am convinced that I should totally fail in any other.'

But the new forces did have a slight effect on the world she depicted. Romanticism, for instance, had produced the Gothic novel, and Jane Austen, with her keen eye for absurdity, delighted in satirizing a taste which, by her day, had become more than a little ridiculous. The circulating libraries were packed with horrors designed to titillate the sensitivities of fashionable young ladies, and fashionable young ladies were an essential part of Jane Austen's world.

She also liked to make fun of the taste for the 'picturesque', which was the name given to a style of landscape-gardening. Like the Gothic novel, it was closely allied to the Romantic Movement, insofar as it was a sort of rebellion against reason and proportion. By the end of the eighteenth century, the informal landscapes that were already prevalent were being dismissed for their 'tender smoothness'. Carefully balanced clumps of trees and rolling lawns were being rejected in favour of a wildly asymmetrical confusion of rugged rocks and rampant vegetation. The new taste's leading theorist, Uvedale Price, wrote that the picturesque should be characterized by 'roughness and . . . sudden variation, joined to . . . irregularity' (see plate 36).

It was a principle that was also applied to building. A truly picturesque country house, for instance, was not a classically symmetrical structure which contrasted with the informality of its grounds, but one which blended with the landscape by being deliberately asymmetrical itself. In effect, picturesque architecture was a development of Horace Walpole's Strawberry Hill, and, sure enough, most of the picturesque houses that were built in the early nineteenth century were imitations of medieval castles not unlike Strawberry Hill in conception, but far more rambling and irregular.

The most popular master of this style was the architect, John Nash, who often worked in close collaboration with the equally popular landscape-gardener, Humphrey Repton ('Smith's place is the admiration of all the country,' says a character in Jane Austen's *Mansfield Park*, 'and it was a mere nothing before Repton took it in hand'). When these two were asked to design a house and its grounds, the landscape was always the starting-point. Repton would suggest his improvements, and would then recommend that Nash should design a building that would accord with them.

In Jane Austen's *Northanger Abbey*, Henry Tilney is a devotee of the picturesque. Catherine Morland, whom he is courting, and who is more than willing to be courted, is an eager convert:

36. Landscape gardening takes on an even more 'natural' look. In this Rowlandson watercolour, *The Country House*, the house itself hides snugly amongst the trees. The gentleman on the left is explaining the principles of the picturesque to his companion, with the help of one of the many books on the subject.

> . . . a lecture on the picturesque followed, in which his instructions
> were so clear that she soon began to see beauty in every thing admired
> by him, and her attention was so earnest, that he became perfectly
> satisfied of her having a great deal of natural taste. . . . Catherine was
> so hopeful a scholar, that when they gained the top of Beechen Cliff,
> she voluntarily rejected the whole city of Bath, as unworthy to make
> part of a landscape.

Bath was still enjoying a reputation as Britain's most fashionable health resort. To many people at the time, it must have
seemed the most beautiful city in the world, a pinnacle of 'civil-
ised' taste. With its immaculately balanced network of colon-
naded crescents, squares and streets, it epitomized classical grace
and proportion (see plate 37). By making Catherine Morland, in
her innocent enthusiasm for the picturesque, dismiss it as 'unworthy' – a patently absurd thing to do – Jane Austen was de-
claring her own preference for the classical tradition, and her
distrust of taking an obviously 'romantic' taste too far.

In the higher reaches of society, the old aristocratic values,
naturally enough, took a while to die out, and the classical tradition was not easily overcome. In fact, in many aspects of taste, the
age of Jane Austen was characterized by a classicism that was
actually more restrained than it had ever been before. In fashion,
for instance, women shed their hooped skirts and their high wigs,
their paint and their powder and their abundant jewellery, for a
far simpler style of dress and coiffure, allowing their hair to be
seen for the first time. Men, too, dismissed wigs as outmoded,
and rejected breeches in favour of tight-fitting pantaloons, wear-
ing high-cut dress-coats so as to accentuate a leaner more mas-
culine shape. Attention-catching flamboyance was no longer
desirable; sobriety and restraint were *de rigeur* (see plate 38).

The graceful unobtrusiveness of the clothes worn by fashionable men and women was in perfect keeping with the predomi-
nantly classical tone of the homes in which they lived and the
streets down which they walked. Earlier in the eighteenth century,
a similar move towards uniformity of taste had taken place in
other things – furniture, ceramics and silver – so that they, too,
would match the simple grace of the buildings they adorned. This

7. A monument to Regency: the Brighton Pavilion.

8. Turbulence and machinery: J. M. W. Turner's *Rain, Steam and Speed*.

9. Celebrating Britain's greatness: *The Great Exhibition* by Thomas Colman Dibden.

37. Lansdowne Crescent, in Bath.

38. 'Restrained' fashion at a London club: a drawing by Cruikshank.

move was largely due to the influence of the architect and interior designer Robert Adam, a man whose impact on taste was so forceful and wide-reaching that the period in which he flourished (roughly between 1760 and 1790) is often named after him.

Before the Age of Adam, the bric-a-brac with which the average wealthy home was filled was dominated by a taste for heavily decorated objects called 'rococo' – a taste which emanated from France, and which derived its name from the French word *rocaille*, which literally meant 'rocky' or 'shell-encrusted'. With the arrival of Adam, however, the rococo waned and was replaced by a modest, classical delicacy, so that a house and the things it contained were given an exquisite harmony of taste (see plate 39).

39. The library at Osterley Park, by Robert Adam. The furniture is delicately suited to the interior as a whole.

Adam himself liked to supervize every aspect of design in the homes he built. If he could help it, nothing – not even the snuff-box on the table – was allowed to escape his meticulous eye. But one did not have to know Adam personally in order to bring the new taste for restraint into one's home. 'Pattern-books', containing examples of items in the Adam-style, were being published with increasing regularity. One of the most influential was George Hepplewhite's *Cabinet-Maker and Upholsterer's Guide*. It was the bible of the new style in furniture, preaching the gospel of Adam to cabinet-makers and their customers all over Britain.

It was also a happy fact that the Age of Adam coincided with the early stages of industrialization. Whilst certain enterprising individuals were improving the output of the necessities of life, men like Matthew Boulton and Josiah Wedgwood were pouring a similar amount of time and energy into the mass-production of 'luxury' goods. Boulton is perhaps best known for his inspired partnership with James Watt in the manufacture of steam-engines, but before he met Watt he had perfected the production of a fusion of copper and silver called silver plate. At his factory in Birmingham, his rolling-mills were capable of making a plate so thin that it could be moulded and assembled quickly and efficiently into a whole variety of articles that looked just like silver, but were of course much cheaper. Boulton found a huge market amongst the rising class of moderately wealthy people already being spawned by the industrial revolution – people who could not afford to indulge themselves quite as lavishly as the gentry, but who were nonetheless anxious to prove themselves as the possessors of good taste. Most of the items produced for these people were in the best Adam style (see plate 40).

At the same time as Boulton, Josiah Wedgwood was appealing to the same market by producing a pottery that was both cheap and acceptably fashionable. In fact, it was so fashionable, that it was bought, not only by the middle classes, but by the very wealthy. The Queen ordered a teaset of Wedgwood creamware in 1765, and allowed Wedgwood to call himself 'Potter to Her Majesty'. A brilliant salesman, he made the most of his new title, and by 1773, the year in which Catherine the Great of Russia

40. A typical design from a Boulton pattern-book.

ordered a 952-piece dinner service, his name was known throughout Europe. His most popular and distinctive product was a form
of pottery called jasperware, characterized by a matt finish
adorned with white figures in low relief (see plate 41). Significantly, it was inspired by one of Robert Adam's favourite
forms of plasterwork.

The influence of pioneers like Hepplewhite, Boulton and
Wedgwood, all of them guided by the spirit of Adam, created a
polished uniformity of taste, unparalleled before or since. But in
the early 1800s, even Adam was thought to be too fanciful and
decorative for the truly discerning palate. Adam had based his
designs on a first-hand study of the domestic buildings and interiors of the ancient Romans, but connoisseurs were now looking

41. Wedgwood jasperware – a vase closely modelled from
an original found at Pompeii.

to Greece rather than to Rome for inspiration. Greece was the
older of the two classical civilizations, and Greek design was
characterized by a stark grandeur that was far simpler and, in the
eyes of a new generation of architects and designers, far purer
than anything the Romans had produced. When one of Adam's

most celebrated successors, Henry Holland, built Carlton House
in London (see plate 42) for the Prince of Wales in the 1780s,
Horace Walpole, now an old man but still very much in touch
with the latest opinions, wrote: 'How sick one shall be after this
chaste palace of Mr Adam's gingerbread and sippets of em-
broidery'.

The 'Greek Revival' was given a boost in 1806 when a con-
noisseur called Lord Elgin started to bring pieces of the Parthenon
in Athens back to London. Suddenly, it seemed, everything had
to be Greek – there must be Greek chairs (see plate 43), Greek
tables, Greek couches, Greek wall-hangings, Greek pottery,
Greek silver, all of them corresponding to the clean simplicity
of the 'chaste palace' in which they were housed.

Most of the classical buildings erected during the years between
the decline of Adam and the Victorian age were indeed 'chaste
palaces', reaching a fine culmination in the stark grandeur of

42. Henry Holland's Carlton House.

43. An immaculately 'Greek' chair.

John Nash's 'improvements' in central London, which he began in 1811. They included a 'Royal Mile' that cut through the town in an uninterrupted sweep, starting at Henry Holland's Carlton House in the south and culminating in a spacious park in the north. The central section of the sweep was called Regent Street, and the park was christened Regent's Park. Much of the glorious arrangement still survives as a monument to this last great phase of classicism known as the Regency (see plate 44).

44. Cumberland Terrace in Regent's Park, designed by John Nash.

Concentrating on the classical aspects of the Regency it is easy to conclude that it was an age in which a feeling for restraint and a distrust of excess inherited from the eighteenth century was brought to a delightful peak of perfection. In many ways, this was certainly the case. But Romanticism was undermining all the accepted tenets, not only in literature and painting, but in architecture and design as well.

There was nothing particularly restrained, after all, about the character of the man after whom the age was named. George, Prince of Wales, did not become Regent until 1811, when his father George III finally gave way to incurable insanity, but he had already dominated the fashionable world for two decades. He was a man quite incapable of frugality, and by the time he became Regent he was in debt to the government to the tune of half a million pounds. The lavish fete which he held in Carlton House to celebrate his inauguration was a clear sign that he intended to continue in the extravagant manner to which he had become accustomed. Shelley observed bitterly:

> It is said that this entertainment will cost £120,000. Nor will it be the last bauble which the nation must buy to amuse this overgrown bantling of Regency.

Two thousand guests were invited to participate in what a lesser, and less discontented, poet, Tom Moore, described as an 'assemblage of beauty, splendour, and profuse magnificence.' The talking-point of the occasion was a stream, filled with live fish, that meandered down the length of the long table, decorated with bridges, tiny water plants, flowers and green banks. Such a piece of indulgence could hardly be called restrained or classical.

The room that housed the feast was not classical either. It was Gothic, as was the feature of Carlton House that was its owner's pride and joy – a huge conservatory, built in the shape of a cathedral, with a nave, two aisles, and a series of vast stained-glass windows (see plate 45). There were signs of other highly unclassical tastes, too, in this building which Walpole had praised for its chasteness and propriety – including a delightful room in the chinese style, packed with bamboo and dragons and the

45. The Gothic conservatory at Carlton House.

figures of mandarins. For his furniture and ornaments, the Prince looked to France. Most of his tables, chests, chairs, clocks, mirrors, pieces of porcelain and tapestries were French, and no expense was spared in getting French cabinet-makers, metal-workers and wood-carvers to work on the interiors directly. To those who visited it, Carlton House must have been an exciting, almost suffocating demonstration of its owner's extraordinarily wide-ranging tastes.

Sadly, it no longer exists. But another of the Prince's pet-projects, the Royal Pavilion at Brighton, does. Before he decided to build a second home there in 1785, Brighton was a small un-prepossessing fishing-town, but, because of the beau monde's frantic anxiety to follow the Prince's example, it rapidly became a resort that rivalled Bath. The original pavilion was a classical building, designed, appropriately, by Henry Holland. But between 1815 and 1818, it underwent an extraordinary trans-formation, under the supervision of John Nash. The Prince had become fascinated by a new taste – not Gothic or classical, but Indian – and Nash obliged by producing a building that, from the outside, resembled an Indian moghul's palace (see colour plate 7). Inside, it reflected a multiplicity of styles. 'How can one des-cribe such a piece of architecture?' wrote the wife of the Russian ambassador, 'The style is a mixture of Moorish, Tartar, Gothic and Chinese, and all in stone and iron.'

Despite the predominance of the classical tradition in Regency taste, the Regent's own use of several styles was a sign of rest-lessness – a feeling of the need to break with that tradition. The influence of the Greeks and the Romans was now only a part of a plethora of tastes, all of them vying with each other to gain the upper hand. Buildings and ornaments were produced in a profuse variety of styles – Gothic, Chinese, Turkish, Indian, Italian Renaissance, French rococo, Greek and Roman.

The way in which Nash was capable of creating not only the Brighton Pavilion, but several picturesquely irregular castles, as well as the severe classicism of Regent's Park and Regent Street, was a sign of a new subservience on the part of architects and designers. They were being asked to turn their hands to virtually anything their patrons required. No longer 'influencing' taste in the way that Adam had done, they now had a duty to work ac-cording to the whims and fancies of those who paid them.

Thomas Sheraton, the most famous furniture designer of the Regency, published his *Cabinet Dictionary* in 1803. It was a book that was obviously produced for a wide and various market and not for the purpose of 'influencing' taste in any way. Sheraton was a dab-hand at designing anything anybody wanted to buy. His work was a rag-bag – a very accomplished one, but a rag-bag nonetheless – of different styles.

In silver, the subservience of the designer to his market was evident in the fact that taste was dominated, not by a particular individual, but by a firm, Rundell, Bridge and Rundell, goldsmiths to the Prince Regent. The standard of craftsmanship in the firm was consistently high – the shoddiness associated with modern mass-production had not yet arrived – but its designs were produced according to order, and its products reflected the individual tastes of individual buyers. It was quite possible to purchase Gothic as well as classical silverware, and the rococo re-emerged with such force that many of the articles produced were almost indistinguishable from those made half-a-century earlier.

In 1821, the Regent was at last crowned King George IV. Parliament paid a quarter of a million pounds for his coronation. The provisions for the celebratory banquet speak for themselves, when we remember what most British people were enduring at the same time:

> 160 tureens of soup, 160 dishes of fish; 160 hot joints, 160 dishes of vegetables; 480 sauce boats (lobster, butter, mint); 80 dishes of braised ham, 80 savoury pies; 80 dishes of goose, 80 of savoury cakes; 80 of braised beef, 80 of braised capons; 1,190 side dishes. 320 dishes of mounted pastry, 320 of small pastry; 400 dishes of jellies and creams; 160 dishes of shellfish (lobster and crayfish); 160 dishes of cold roast fowl, 80 of cold lamb.

George IV reigned for nine years. He was an unpopular king, not of course amongst his fashionable followers, but certainly amongst the people as a whole. When he died in 1830, a friend of Lord Byron observed, walking home from parliament: 'I saw nothing like grief or joy, only a bustle in the streets.' The bustle was the sound of approaching democracy.

Four years after George IV's death, and two years after that great political watershed the Reform Bill, the old Palace of

Westminster, containing the Houses of Parliament, was almost completely destroyed by fire. The rebuilding of Westminster Palace, the constitutional centre of a thriving nation, was a matter of urgency, and a parliamentary committee was formed to discuss the matter of style. Until then, despite the confusion of styles now evident in private homes, it had never been questioned that public buildings – town halls, banks, government offices and such – should remain firmly classical, and it was assumed by many that the most important public building in the land would follow that tradition. But when, in 1835, the committee held a competition in which architects were asked to submit their recommendations, the winning design, by a young architect called Charles Barry, was unerringly Gothic (see plate 46).

It was a highly significant move, for it marked the final over-throw of a style that had dominated British taste for over a century, just as the Reform Bill which preceded it undermined the assumption on the part of the aristocratic landowners that they were the only men with a God-given right to run the country. The classical tradition was an essentially *aristocratic* one. It had

46. Charles Barry's Houses of Parliament.

47. *Pentonville by Sunset* by John O'Connor: the Gothic shadow looming in the background is St. Pancras Station.

been created and championed by the men whose tasteful homes still adorned the British countryside. Once the first important step had been made towards true democracy, it was only natural that this tradition should no longer prevail.

In the Regency battle of styles, the main combatants had always been the classical and the Gothic. The multitude of other tastes never seriously challenged the precedence of those two in the fight for supremacy. With the re-building of the Houses of Parliament, Gothic, which had been challenging classicism ever since Walpole had built Strawberry Hill, finally won. It towered over the Victorian era, symbolizing the excited aspirations of a new age (see plate 47). But its influence was never as strong or as all-embracing as that of classicism. There was no rule of taste any more. Freedom was the watchword here, just as it was in politics, in literature, in painting. And so, from the graceful regularity of the eighteenth-century interior, taste arrived at the packed clutter and confusion of the Victorian sitting-room. Was it a regrettable collapse, or a thrilling free-for-all, filled with possibilities? People have been arguing about that ever since it happened. Finally, the answer can only be based on personal preference. It is, as we say, *a matter of taste*.

𑁍𑁍𑁍𑁍𑁍𑁍

# VICTORIAN HOPES AND FEARS

𑁍𑁍𑁍𑁍𑁍𑁍

IN Turner's *Rain Steam and Speed* (see colour plate 8), painted in 1844, the storm which was brewing in the background of Gainsborough's portrait of Mr and Mrs Andrews has well and truly broken. The rain pelts the landscape into obscurity, covering it with a frenzied whirl of colour which reflects the dizzy turbulence of a new age. Mr and Mrs Andrews dominate Gainsborough's painting just as they and their kind dominated the society of which they were a part. In Turner's picture, though, the dominant feature, the centre from which the rest emanates, is not human, but a machine – a railway-engine, in fact, black, busy and smoky.

In an essay called *Signs of the Times*, Thomas Carlyle called his age an 'age of machinery', and he excitedly echoed what must have been the feelings of many early Victorians as they considered the advance of mechanization:

> Nothing can resist us, we war with rude Nature; and, by our resistless engines, come off always victorious, and loaded with spoils.

But Carlyle was too deep a thinker to be blindly optimistic about his times, and his essay expressed profound fears as well as hopes. The nub of its argument was this: quite apart from producing the railway and the power-loom and a host of other vital inventions

> the mechanical genius of our time has diffused itself into quite other provinces. Not the external and physical alone is now managed by machinery, but the internal and spiritual also . . .

In other words, the passion for mechanization was not only sub-
stituting machine power for human labour, but was creating a
society in which *people themselves* were being turned into, and
treated as, machines. Coleridge had been thinking along the same
lines as Carlyle when he wrote of a 'population being mechanized
into engines for the manufacture of the new rich men'.

Such a tendency was most immediately evident in the field of
education. In the first half of the nineteenth century, thousands
of day schools, with the help of voluntary subscription, were
established in the industrial towns and in many rural districts,
and it was estimated that by 1850 about three quarters of the
child population of Britain was receiving some form of rudi-
mentary schooling. In itself, that is an impressive statistic, but
we have to remember that many of the new school children did
not attend for longer than a year, and none of them stayed at
school beyond the age of eleven. As for the standard of education
received, a child was usually thought adequately 'educated' if he
or she could recite certain selected passages by heart. Children
did not learn to understand what they were reading, let alone
enjoy the process. To begin with, the curriculum was restricted
to the scriptures, but even when it was widened to include other
subjects, such as science and Latin, the method of learning remained dull and mechanical. The introduction of monitors,
selected from amongst the older pupils, made the process even
more impersonal and machine-like (see plate 48). In fact, the
founder of the monitorial system, Joseph Lancaster, proudly
referred to his invention as a 'mechanical system of education'.
Andrew Bell, the inventor of a system not unlike Lancaster's,
called his scheme 'the STEAM ENGINE of the MORAL WORLD',
thereby admitting that he thought of schools as being little
more than educational factories, designed for the rapid and
efficient production of a minimum standard of knowledge and
literacy. The whole arrangement seemed to be prompted by a
single cruel purpose: to get the children back into the true factories as quickly as possible, for it was in the true factories that
their primary duty lay. They were indeed being 'mechanized into
engines'.

48. Monitors and master at work in a Victorian school.

Bell and Lancaster worked under the spell of a philosophy that was almost a religion in Victorian days – the philosophy of Utilitarianism. Its originator, Jeremy Bentham, had first formulated his ideas in the 1770s. He was an atheist and a true democrat. He did not believe in laws laid down by God since the beginning of time; he believed in liberty and in the right of every individual to do with his own life as he saw fit. The only law by which a man should govern his actions was the law of what Bentham called 'the greatest happiness of the greatest number'. Any action which could be seen to hinder the progress towards this goal was to be discouraged – he called it a 'mischievous' act. Conversely, an act which contributed to the achievement of 'the greatest happiness' was an act of 'utility', or a 'useful' act. It was a simple and attractive philosophy, but the trouble was that Bentham, who was not a very imaginative man, thought of happiness only in terms of *material* well-being – a man, he said, could be considered happy if he had a roof over his head and enough to eat and not much else. Spiritual, 'inner' happiness had no part to play in his rather dry view of the world. So he dismissed works of the imagination and the arts in general as being 'mischievous', because he could not see how they served a useful purpose in a society dedicated to the pursuit of physical contentment. In a style typical of his arid prose, he described them as 'anergastic (no-work-producing)'.

True to the spirit of Bentham, the schools designed for the education of working-class children had no poetry or fiction on their shelves. 'Teach these boys and girls nothing but Facts,' says the schoolmaster Thomas Gradgrind in Charles Dickens' novel *Hard Times*, 'Facts alone are wanted in this life. Plant nothing else, and root out everything else.' The forbidden word in the Gradgrind school is the word 'Fancy': 'You must discard the word Fancy altogether.' *Hard Times* is Dickens' angriest novel, and the great novelist spared none of his satirical fury in attacking a system of education which seemed to have no room for fantasy or beauty or excitement or joy of any kind. But he saw Utilitarianism as a sickness which spread far beyond the confines of the schoolroom. The Gradgrind school is part of an industrial community called Coketown – and Dickens described Coketown as 'a triumph of fact' without a 'taint of fancy in it':

> It contained several large streets all very like one another, and many small streets still more like one another, inhabited by people equally like one another, who all went in and out at the same hours, with the same sound upon the same pavements, to do the same work, and to whom every day was the same as yesterday and tomorrow, and every year the counterpart of the last and the next.

The inhabitants of this drab 'town of machinery' yearn for some form of brief escape, for some colour in their lives, 'some relaxation, encouraging good humour and good spirits'. But Coketown is the very antithesis of colour or relaxation or enjoyment of any kind. 'You saw nothing in Coketown but what was severely workful.'

Although no community of living thinking people could possibly be as bleak as the one Dickens depicted, his exaggerations were not that far from the truth. In a book called *Stubborn Facts from the Factories*, a Manchester cotton worker quoted from the rule book of a particular mill:

> If any hand in the mill is seen *talking* to another, *whistling*, or *singing*, will be fined sixpence . . .

And the same worker wrote:

> In some mills, the crime of sitting down to take a little rest is visited with a penalty of *one shilling*.

In 1850, one shilling was almost a day's wage – a high price indeed to pay for a moment's respite. This was Utilitarianism taken to a merciless extreme – talking, whistling, singing and sitting down were not 'useful', therefore they were not allowed. It was horribly true that virtually every waking moment of a worker's active life was dedicated to the service of the factory and its machinery. Holidays were virtually unheard of. A weekend was a Saturday afternoon. Engels wrote bitterly:

> The operative is condemned to let his physical and mental powers decay in this utter monotony, it is his mission to be bored every day and all day long from his eighth year.

Utilitarian values were so powerful in Victorian Britain because they suited the opinions of the expanding 'middle class', and the middle class had replaced the landowning gentry as the nation's masters. The gentry still existed, of course, sending their sons to the great public schools, entertaining each other at their country houses, fighting for places in parliament just as their ancestors had done. In fact, in 1850, despite the Reform Bill, most seats in the House of Commons were still occupied by land-owners. But although the gentry enjoyed considerable political influence, they no longer set the tone culturally in the manner of their eighteenth-century predecessors. The whole spirit of a brash, competitive, town-dwelling age was against them. It was now in the hands of Coleridge's 'new rich men' – a classification which included not only the moneyed manufacturers but those who depended on them for their livelihood, who admired their success and followed their example: bankers, civil servants, accountants, commercial travellers, engineers, technicians, doc-tors, teachers and lawyers.

The members of the middle class believed in individual initia-tive, in thrift and sobriety, and, above all, in hard work. Their goal was wealth, justly and diligently earned. To many of them, time spent in relaxing for the sake of it, in reading, or looking at pictures, or listening to music, was time wasted. Their attitude was immaculately summarized by a writer in the Utilitarian *Westminster Review*, who asked the telling question: 'how the universal pursuit of literature and poetry, is to conduce towards cotton-spinning.' The poet Matthew Arnold called them 'philis-tines'. The Philistines were originally a tribe in South West Palestine, enemies of the Israelites. As Arnold explained:

> Philistine . . . originally meant . . . a strong, dogged, unenlightened opponent of the chosen people, of the children of light . . . We have not the expression in English. Perhaps we have not the word because we have so much of the thing.

Philistinism was the worship of wealth and material progress at the expense of any regard for wider more spiritual virtues such as the cultivation of beauty and feeling and the imagination – for 'culture' in general. This is how Arnold defined culture:

Culture looks beyond machinery, culture hates hatred, culture has
one great passion, the passion for sweetness and light.

To Arnold, a society without culture, however prosperous and
successful it might be, was nothing more than a barren waste-
land, and Victorian Britain, the wealthiest nation in the world,
was in grave danger of becoming just that.

Not all members of the middle class were as hostile to the
imagination and to culture as Arnold liked to think. After all,
where did he, and Dickens, and all the other great Victorian
novelists and poets, find their audience, if not amongst the class
they so often denounced? It is important to remember that the
'philistines' were also the new reading public, hungry for poetry
and novels, creating a market larger than any writer had ever
enjoyed before. And the Utilitarian eagerness to 'educate' the
lower orders into a modicum of 'useful' knowledge made the
Victorian era an age, not only of free schools, but of libraries,
institutes of adult education, and museums – all of them open to
all comers. Our own society owes too much to the Victorians for
us to dismiss them all as unfeeling wealth-worshippers.

Nonetheless, many Victorian intellectuals sensed a prevailing
bleakness about their age which made them deeply pessimistic.
Some – including Arnold – recognized a threat to the spiritual
happiness of the nation that was even more serious than philistinism. It was a threat which came from the realm of science.
Various geologists and naturalists had begun to suggest that the
earth and the things on it had not, as the bible stated, been
created in six days, but had actually evolved gradually over
millions of years, through a process which they called 'the struggle
for existence'. It was a struggle in which all forms of life fought
pitilessly for survival – in which the strong survived and the weak
went under. Man, they implied, far from being given his supremacy over the other species by divine right, had also been a part
of this fight. Such a theory completely undermined the eighteenth-century idea of a 'Scale of Being'. What frightened those
who first encountered it was the implication that God seemed to
have had no part in the creation of the world or of man. Either
He was blind to the murderous ways of nature, or else – and this

was a truly terrible prospect to those who sensed it first – He did not exist at all. *On the Origin of Species* by Charles Darwin, published in 1859, was the clearest and most influential expression of the evolutionary theory. But certain Victorians were disturbed by the implications of evolution before they knew about Darwin. The poet Tennyson was one. His greatest work, *In Memoriam*, published in 1850, revealed a cold loneliness and uncertainty which would have made even the most despairing of the Romantics shudder:

> I falter where I firmly trod,
>> And falling with my weight of cares
>> Upon the great world's altar-stairs
> That slope through darkness up to God
> I stretch lame hands of faith and grope,
>> And gather dust and chaff . . .

Most Victorians – particularly middle-class Victorians – were more actively religious than their eighteenth-century predecessors. No self-respecting family would let a Sunday pass without attending church at least once, and family prayers were a daily ritual. But these strict observances were perhaps merely efforts to keep darker thoughts at bay. Arnold felt that his contemporaries were trying to 'shut off from themselves the intellectual current which they fear might carry them away to the shores of desolation.' And in his fine poem *Dover Beach*, he summed up, with an aching sadness, what he felt to be the true nature of his times:

> The Sea of Faith
> Was once, too, at the full, and round earth's shore
> Lay like the folds of a bright girdle furl'd.
> But now I only hear
> Its melancholy, long, withdrawing roar,
> Retreating, to the breath
> Of the night-wind, down the vast edges drear
> And naked shingles of the world.

Had the spirit of progress, the relentless search for the new in all things, the whole tempestuous ferment, really been worth it, if all it could finally show for its efforts was such a wretched emptiness of the spirit? To those who had the time and the will to reflect on such things, the mid-nineteenth century often seemed a barren age indeed, and the world of a hundred years before took on the distant gleam of a lost paradise.

But most Victorians did not think too hard, and for them the dominant feeling was one of unabashed optimism. Even the deep thinkers could occasionally reveal high hopes. Here is Tennyson in one of his happier moments:

> For I dipt into the future, far as human eye could see,
> Saw the Vision of the world, and all the wonder that would be . . .

The Great Exhibition of 1851, held in London's Hyde Park, in a building justly called the Crystal Palace, was a tremendous affirmation of this spirit of hope (see colour plate 9). 4,500 tons of iron and 400 tons of glass were the essential components of a structure that was 2,784 feet long, 408 feet broad and 108 feet in height. The whole thing took a mere six months to build. The Exhibition's full title was 'the Exhibition of the Works of Industry of All Nations', but its main purpose seems to have been to celebrate Britain's commercial and technological superiority over other lands. It was a magnificent paean to the Industrial Revolution. Six million people visited the Crystal Palace. A few came from abroad, but most were British, and they formed a fair cross-section of British society at the time – all classes, all occupations, and from all corners of the country. Most of them had come by rail. Henry Mayhew observed:

> You see the farmers, their dusty hats telling the distance they have come, with their mouths wide agape, leaning over the bars to see the self-acting mills at work (see plate 49).

Prince Albert, who had masterminded the entire venture, expressed the age's optimism in his speech at the Exhibition's opening:

> It is our heartfelt prayer that this undertaking, which has for its end the promotion of all branches of human industry, and the strengthening of the bonds of peace and friendship among all nations of the earth, may, by the blessing of Divine Providence, help the welfare of

49. Machinery at the Great Exhibition.

Your Majesty's people, and be long remembered among the brightest circumstances of Your Majesty's peaceful and happy reign.

And Queen Victoria recorded in her journal that evening:

God bless my dearest Albert, and my dear country, which has shown itself so great today.

In that memorable year, the novelist and historian Charles Kingsley, one of the age's most robust optimists, wrote:

Look around you and see what is the characteristic of your country and your generation at this moment. What a yearning, what an expectation. . . ! Your very costermonger trolls out his belief that 'there's a good time coming!'

It is difficult to believe that the cotton worker, labouring in the dim confines of the factory, would have joined the happy costermonger in his cry. But it had almost certainly entered his consciousness that a better and happier world was attainable, perhaps even only round the corner – if not for him, at least for his children. Bright possibilities may have seemed distant, but nonetheless they were in the air, only waiting to be caught.

꽤꽤꽤꽤꽤

# BIBLIOGRAPHY

꽤꽤꽤꽤꽤

## I. SOURCE MATERIAL

Altick, R. D. *The English Common Reader, A Social History of the Mass Reading Public 1800–1900*. University of Chicago Press, Chicago & London, 1957
Ashton, T. R. *The Industrial Revolution*. Oxford University Press, Oxford, 1968
Bate, W. Jackson. *From Classic to Romantic*. Harper and Row, New York, 1961
Briggs, Asa. *Victorian Cities*. Penguin, Harmondsworth, 1968
Burton, Anthony. *Josiah Wedgwood*. André Deutsch, London, 1977
Burton, Anthony. *Remains of a Revolution*. André Deutsch, London, 1975
Burton, Elizabeth. *The Georgians at Home*. Arrow, London, 1973
Burton, Elizabeth. *The Early Victorians at Home*. Arrow, London, 1974
Clark, Kenneth. *The Gothic Revival*. Murray, London, 1962
Clark, Kenneth. *The Romantic Rebellion*. Murray, London, 1973
Cole, G. D. H. and Postgate, R. *The Common People*. Methuen, London, 1961
Cook, Olive. *The English Country House*. Thames and Hudson, London, 1974
Ford, Boris (Ed.). *From Blake to Byron*. Penguin, Harmondsworth, 1962
Furneaux Jordan, R. *Victorian Architecture*. Penguin, Harmondsworth, 1966
Furst, Lilian R. *Romanticism in Perspective*. Macmillan, London, 1969
Harvie C., Martin G., and Scharf A. *Industrialisation and Culture*. Macmillan, 1975
Hibbert, Christopher. *George IV*. Penguin, Harmondsworth, 1976
Hobsbawm, E. J. *The Age of Revolution*. Sphere, London, 1973
Houghton, Walter E. *The Victorian Frame of Mind*. Yale University Press, New Haven, 1957
Jarrett, Derek. *England in the Age of Hogarth*. Paladin, St. Albans, 1976
Jenkins, Elizabeth. *Jane Austen*. Sphere, London, 1973
Klingender, F. *Art and the Industrial Revolution*. Paladin, London, 1972
Lister, R. G. *British Romantic Art*. Bell, London, 1973
Perkin, Harold. *The Age of the Railway*. Panther, London, 1970
Piper, David. *Painting in England 1500–1880*. Penguin, Harmondsworth, 1965
Plumb, J. H. *England in the Eighteenth Century*. Penguin, Harmondsworth, 1950

Priestley, J. B. *The Prince of Pleasure*. Sphere, London, 1971

Quennell, Peter. *Romantic England*. Weidenfeld and Nicolson, London, 1970

Royston Pike, E. *Human Documents of Adam Smith's Time*. Allen and Unwin, London, 1974

Royston Pike, E. *Human Documents of the Industrial Revolution*. Allen and Unwin, London, 1966

Steegman, John. *The Rule of Taste*. Macmillan, London, 1968

Summerson, John. *Architecture in Britain 1530–1830*. Penguin, Harmondsworth, 1969

Thompson, E. P. *The Making of the English Working Class*. Penguin, Harmondsworth, 1968

Thomson, David. *England in the Nineteenth Century*. Penguin, Harmondsworth, 1950

Tomalin, Claire. *Mary Wollstonecraft*. Penguin, Harmondsworth, 1967

Trevelyan, G. M. *English Social History*. Penguin, Harmondsworth, 1967

Vicinus, Martha. *The Industrial Muse*. Croom Helm, London, 1974

Williams, Raymond. *Culture and Society*. Penguin, Harmondsworth, 1963

Williams, Raymond. *The Long Revolution*. Penguin, Harmondsworth, 1965

Wintersgill, Donald. *The Guardian Book of Antiques*. Collins, London, 1975

Yglesias, J. C. R. *London Life and the Great Exhibition*. Longmans, London, 1964

## 2. LITERATURE OF THE TIME

Austen, Jane. *Mansfield Park*. Penguin, Harmondsworth, 1966

Austen, Jane. *Northanger Abbey*. Penguin, Harmondsworth, 1972

Burke, Edmund. *Reflections on the Revolution in France*. Penguin, Harmondsworth, 1969

Carlyle, Thomas. *Selected Writings*. Penguin, Harmondsworth, 1971

Cobbett, William. *Rural Rides*. Penguin, Harmondsworth, 1967

Darwin, Charles. On the *Origin of Species*. Penguin, Harmondsworth, 1968

Davison, Denis (Ed.). *Eighteenth Century English Verse*. Penguin, Harmondsworth, 1973

Defoe, Daniel. *A Tour through the Whole Island of Great Britain*. Penguin, Harmondsworth, 1971

Dickens, Charles. *Hard Times*. Penguin, Harmondsworth, 1969

Engels, Friedrich. *The Condition of the Working Class in England*. Panther, London, 1969

Fielding, Henry. *Tom Jones*. Penguin, Harmondsworth, 1966

Gaskell, Elizabeth. *North and South*. Penguin, Harmondsworth, 1970

Hazlitt, William. *Selected Writings*. Penguin, Harmondsworth, 1970

Keats, John. *Selected Letters*. Oxford University Press, Oxford, 1970

MacBeth, George (Ed.). *Victorian Verse*. Penguin, Harmondsworth, 1969

Malthus, Thomas. *An Essay on the Principle of Population.* Penguin, Harmonds-worth, 1970

Paine, Thomas. *The Rights of Man.* Penguin, Harmondsworth, 1969

Ruskin, John. *Ruskin Today* (ed. Kenneth Clark). Penguin, Harmondsworth, 1967

Scott, Walter. *Ivanhoe.* Everyman, Dent, London, 1906

Smith, Adam. *The Wealth of Nations.* Penguin, Harmondsworth, 1970

Sterne, Laurence. *Tristram Shandy.* Penguin, Harmondsworth, 1967

Walpole, Horace. *Selected Letters.* Everyman, Dent, London, 1926

Walpole, Horace, Beckford, William and Shelley, Mary. *Three Gothic Novels.* Penguin, Harmondsworth, 1968

Wordsworth, Dorothy. *Journals.* Oxford University Press, Oxford, 1971

Wright, David (Ed.). *English Romantic Verse.* Penguin, Harmondsworth, 1968

3. FICTION FOR THE SAME AGE GROUP

Bibby, Violet. *Tinner's Quest.* Faber, London, 1977

Burton, Hester. *Time of Trial.* Oxford University Press, London, 1963

Faulkner, John Meads. *Moonfleet.* Penguin, Puffin Books, Harmondsworth, 1970

Garfield, Leon. *Black Jack.* Longman, London, 1968 and Penguin, Puffin Books, Harmondsworth, 1971

Hunt, Irene. *Across Five Aprils.* The Bodley Head, London, 1965 and Heine-mann Education, London, 1969

McGregor, Iona. *The Burning Hill.* Faber, London, 1970

McGregor, Iona. *Tree of Liberty.* Faber, London, 1972

Schlee, Ann. *Ask Me No Questions.* Macmillan, London, 1976

Trease, Geoffrey. *Comrades for the Charter.* Brockhampton, Leicester, 1972

Trease, Geoffrey. *The Thunder of Valmy.* Macmillan, London, 1960

Trease, Geoffrey. *Violet for Bonaparte.* Macmillan, London, 1976

Welch, Ronald. *Escape from France.* Oxford University Press, London, 1969

# INDEX